Fish

Christian Teubner

Fish

BARRON'S

Woodbury, New York • London • Toronto • Sydney

First English-language edition published 1986 by
Barron's Educational Series, Inc.
© 1985 by Grafe und Unzer GmbH, Munich, West Germany

The title of the German edition is *Fisch*.

All inquiries should be addressed to:
Barron's Educational Series, Inc.
113 Crossways Park Drive
Woodbury, New York 11797

Library of Congress Catalog Card No. 86-3374

International Standard Book No. 0-8120-5733-3

Library of Congress Cataloging-in-Publication Data

Teubner, Christian.
    Fish.

    Translation of: Fisch.
    Includes index.
    1. Cookery (Fish)   I. Title.
TX747.T4813 1986   641.6'92   86-3374
ISBN 0-8120-5733-3

Color photographs by Christian Teubner

Translation and Americanization by Patricia Connell

PRINTED IN HONG KONG

6789   987654321

CONTENTS

BASICS OF FISH COOKERY

Fish is becoming ever more popular, and this picture cookbook of delicious recipes is meant to provide you with lots of ideas for preparing it. Fortunately, the times are long gone when only a few types of fish were considered suitable for eating and when cooking methods were limited to poaching and frying.

Fish is an exceedingly healthful food, much valued for its protein and mineral (particularly iodine) content. As more and more varieties are being sold nowadays, a correspondingly wide array of flavorful new combinations and preparation techniques have come into use.

Tempting new recipes as well as classic favorites are collected in this cookbook, all carefully tested and easy to follow. Any tricky steps are shown in step-by-step photographs. Numerous hints and tips will show you the way to perfect results, and the lavish color photos will whet your appetite and curiosity.

Contemporary fish cookery takes advantage of what is freshest and best in the market. For this reason, the chapters of this book were arranged not by fish type but according to cooking method—poached and steamed, deep-fried, grilled, sautéed, oven-baked, or cooked in a roasting bag, as well as cooked in soup or marinated. Seafoods such as shrimp and mussels round out the selection of both traditional and new recipes. If you cannot find the exact fish called for, many of the recipes suggest other types that can be prepared in the same way — and the Index lists all the varieties used in the book, so that you can find a recipe to suit whatever fish you have.

Buying Fish

The first step in purchasing fish is to familiarize yourself with what is available. Saltwater fish, shellfish, and crustaceans, in particular, are harvested only during certain seasons, and when a fish is most abundant in the market it will naturally be less expensive than at other times of year. This is taken into consideration in this book; usually alternatives are suggested in case the kind of fish called for in the recipe is not available. A fish can nearly always be replaced by another of a similar type if it is more abundant or of better quality — for instance, in a recipe calling for cod you might substitute haddock or perch.

If it turns out that you will have to keep the fish refrigerated for longer than you expected — perhaps for a day or two — you should learn to be flexible about its preparation. In this case it would be wise to bake the fish with vegetables or herbs rather than to poach it with a light sauce, a treatment that should be reserved only for the best and freshest selections.

The question comes up again and again as to whether today's fish are bringing toxic substances (particularly mercury) to our tables from the water in which they were caught. Scientists have found that overall there is little risk, though some varieties of freshwater and predatory fish do contain higher levels of pollutants than most saltwater and nonpredatory species. In any event, commercially caught fish undergo government inspection before arriving at the market.

The Importance of Freshness

Fish should smell as fresh and pleasant as ocean air. A freshwater variety should ideally be purchased as soon as it is killed; the best markets keep the fish alive in tanks until they are sold. A visual inspection will also reveal the fish's freshness. Whole fish should have pink gills that lie flat. The eyes should be clear and protruding, never milky or sunken. If you buy the fish in pieces or fillets, make sure the flesh is firm and glossy, without any dried-out edges or discoloration. Modern refrigeration tecnniques can keep ocean fish fresh for up to two days during its transport inland.

Though serious fish lovers may reject frozen fish on principle, there is no denying that it saves time and effort. For best quality it should be frozen right on the boat from which it was caught. Avoid fish that has thawed in the market; it generally has little flavor.

Modern Methods with Fish

Whole freshwater and small whole saltwater fish should be gutted as soon as possible after purchase, as their digestive organs contain enzymes that hasten spoilage. Most shellfish and crustaceans are sold either still alive or, suitable for some dishes, already cooked. Live crustaceans like shrimp and prawns should be dropped into rapidly boiling water and kept submerged for five minutes with a spoon or skimmer. To cook shellfish such as mussels, see the recipes on pages 12 and 88.

The preparation of whole fish or fillets is described in detail in the corresponding recipes. You need not go as far as radical *nouvelle cuisine* chefs who cook fish so briefly that it is still more or less raw at the bone. But in general these chefs have the right idea: If it is to be optimally juicy and flavorful, fish should be cooked as briefly as possible. Test it often for firmness with the touch of a finger; just half a minute too much cooking can make a critical difference. Frozen fish must be cooked with equal care if it is to still be moist.

Modern cooks also follow explicit rules about handling and seasoning fish. In the past, there were unpardonable mistakes made in preparation. Traditional German cooks, for instance, invariably kept to the "three S" rule — *säubern, säuern, salzen*, or "clean, acidulate (with vinegar), salt" — too often with good reason, because the fish was not always the freshest.

Fresh fish should be rinsed under cold running water ever so briefly, as its tender flesh is very delicate. If it is acidulated at all, it should be with fresh lemon juice (or, if you prefer the flavor, with lime juice) and using a gentle touch. This nicely complements the flavor of most fish — but in turn the acidulating step tends to mask the fish's own flavor, so it is by no means essential for seasoning. The same is true of salt. If necessary, the fish can be lightly and carefully salted, though ocean fish often has a high enough sodium content of its own. In any event, the salting should be done just before cooking, since salt draws out natural moisture and if sprinkled on too far ahead may make the flesh somewhat dry.

The Proper Ingredients

Fine, fresh fish demands the best ingredients: Be choosy in selecting vegetables, butter, oil and so on to ensure success with the final result. Any wine used for cooking should also be of the best quality, especially if the dish is delicately seasoned. Decide ahead of time whether you want the fish's own flavor or that of the seasonings to predominate. This book includes both kinds of dishes — some for purists who like the subtle taste of the fish left unadorned, and some for those who prefer zesty flavors.

And as for seasonings, you will get the best results with fresh herbs. That fish also combines well with onion and garlic is demonstrated in many Mediterranean and Oriental specialties. Just as the wine used for cooking should be of excellent quality, so should the wine served at the table; the best choice is a dry, high-acid white, and lightly sparkling is perfect. Some adventurous diners also like to serve fish with a light red wine from time to time; in this case don't cook with a white wine.

A Shortcut

Many of the recipes in this book begin with a whole, undressed fish. You will save considerable time and effort if you buy fish fillets or a whole fish that has already been cleaned and scaled. You cannot do this for every recipe, of course; some use the fish trimming as a foundation for a stock or sauce. But should you wish to purchase fillets, calculate approximately $1/3$ to $1/2$ pound of skinless and boneless fillets per serving or ask your fish merchant for the equivalent quantity in fillets.

FISH STOCK — FISH SOUPS

Fish Stock

Clear fish stock is virtually indispensable to fine cooking. While it is the basis for numerous fish sauces and soups, it is perhaps most important as a poaching medium.

You will often find yourself with trimmings (skin, bones, and head) after preparing fish, or you can get them at the fish market. Do not use the trimmings of fatty fish such as carp, mackerel, or eel; they will give the broth an oily taste.

Makes about 1 quart (950 mL)
2¼ pounds (1kg) trimmings from fish such as sole, turbot, haddock, or cod
2 medium leeks (white part only)
1 stalk celery
1 bay leaf
1 sprig thyme
2 large shallots
1 clove garlic
3 tablespoons white peppercorns
3 juniper berries
1 whole clove
1 cup (240 mL) dry white wine
3 tablespoons dry vermouth
1 quart (950 mL) water
To clarify
4 ounces (125 g) boneless beef round
4 ounces (125 g) fish fillets
1 leek
1 stalk celery
1 carrot
1 tomato
1 onion
1 clove garlic
1 sprig thyme
¼ bay leaf
3 juniper berries
4 egg whites
6 ice cubes
Salt and freshly ground pepper

Photo 1: Soak fish trimmings in cold water for about 30 minutes to give broth a fresher taste. Clean leeks and celery and tie into bouquet garni with bay leaf and thyme. Peel shallots and chop finely. Measure out unpeeled garlic, spices, wine, and vermouth.

Photo 2: Place fish trimmings and bouquet garni in large saucepan or Dutch oven. Add chopped shallots, garlic, peppercorns, crushed juniper berries, clove, water, wine and vermouth. Bring to simmer. Let mixture simmer for 20 minutes, skimming frequently.

Photo 3: Strain stock through sieve lined with muslin or several layers of cheesecloth, pressing lightly on solids to extract all liquid. Let cool.

Photo 4: If the stock needs to be clarified, grind beef and fish fillets through coarse disk of meat grinder. Slice leek into rings; chop celery, carrot, and tomato. Peel and halve onion. Combine all these ingredients in large saucepan with unpeeled garlic clove, thyme, bay leaf, juniper berries, egg whites, and ice cubes.

Photo 5: Pour 1 cup (240 mL) cold fish stock over the clarifying mixture and mix well. Gradually stir in remaining stock. Place over medium heat and heat through, stirring constantly.

Photo 6: Line sieve with muslin or several layers of cheesecloth and set over large bowl. Pour in stock mixture and let drain thoroughly, but do not press on solids or stock will be cloudy. Season stock with salt and pepper. Use immediately or cool and refrigerate or freeze.

Clear Fish Broth with Vegetables

A concentrated fish stock is known in culinary circles as *fumet* or *fond,* and the better the fish, the better the stock will be. It is not absolutely necessary to use mullet and turbot; a fine stock can also be made from other saltwater or freshwater fish.

4 servings
1 mullet or perch (about 1 pound/400 to 500 g)
1 small turbot or halibut (1 generous pound/500 g)
7 ounces (200 g) cooked and shelled shrimp or prawns
For the broth
2 medium leeks (white part only)
1 carrot
2 stalks celery
1 teaspoon salt
1/2 teaspoon peppercorns
1 bunch Italian parsley
1 cup (240 mL) dry white wine
For the vegetables
7 ounces (200 g) cauliflower
2 medium carrots
2 stalks celery
11/2 tablespoons (20 g) butter
1 tablespoon minced onion
1 cup shelled peas
1 tablespoon chopped fresh parsley
A few chopped tarragon leaves
Salt and freshly ground pepper

Clean fish and rinse under running water. Scale mullet by scraping with dull side of knife from tail toward head; trim away fins with kitchen shears. Cut away head and tail and cut fish into slices about 3/4 inch (2 cm) thick. Fillet the turbot.

Combine all fish trimmings in large saucepan, cover with cold water, and let soak 10 minutes; drain. Return trimmings to pot, add 6 cups (11/2 L) fresh water, and bring to simmer. Meanwhile, clean leek and halve lengthwise; cut carrot and celery into sticks. Add to fish trimmings with salt, peppercorns, and parsley. Bring to broil, then reduce heat and warm gently for 10 minutes. Add wine and heat gently another 10 minutes. Strain fish stock through fine sieve. Return to cleaned saucepan and cook over very low heat until reduced to 4 cups (950 mL).

Separate cauliflower into small florets. Blanch in large amount of boiling salted water until crisp-tender, 8 to 10 minutes; drain. Cut carrots and celery into fine julienne. Melt butter in large saucepan, add onion, and sauté until tender. Add prepared vegetables and peas, and sauté 2 to 3 minutes, stirring.

Add half of fish stock, fish pieces, and shrimp and continue cooking over low heat 6 to 8 minutes. Sprinkle with chopped herbs and add remaining fish stock. Season to taste with salt and pepper.

Smoked Fish and Barley Soup

Photo, top

4 servings
1/2 cup medium barley
1/2 medium onion
1/2 large celery root
1 large leek
2 tablespoons vegetable oil
5 cups (1 1/4 L) fish or meat stock
Salt and freshly ground pepper
2 tablespoons finely chopped fresh herbs (parsley, marjoram, and lovage or celery leaves)
8 ounces (250 g) smoked halibut or other smoked fish

Soak barley in cold water to cover generously at least 6 hours, preferably overnight.

Drain barley. Peel and mince onion. Clean and chop celery root and leek. Heat oil in large saucepan and sauté onion until tender. Add celery root, leek, and stock with softened barley. Cook until barley is tender, 1 to 1 1/2 hours.

Stir in chopped herbs and skinned, boned, and coarsely shredded smoked fish, and cook over low heat 5 to 10 minutes longer.

Potato-Mussel Soup

Photo, bottom

4 servings
2 generous pounds (1 kg) mussels
1 small onion
2 small carrots
2 stalks celery
Salt
1 cup (240 mL) dry white wine
1 cup (240 mL) water
4 large baking potatoes
1 tablespoon minced onion
Freshly ground pepper
1 bunch watercress
1/2 scant cup (100 mL) crème fraîche

Thoroughly scrub and debeard mussels, discarding any with opened shells. Peel and quarter onion. Coarsely chop carrots and celery. Combine onion, carrots, and celery in large saucepan. Add mussels and 1 teaspoon salt, then pour in wine and water. Cover and place over high heat until all mussels have opened, about 10 minutes. Remove from heat and let stand, covered, for 15 minutes. Drain mussels; strain broth through filter paper to remove any sand. Shell mussels and set aside.

Peel and finely dice potatoes. Place in saucepan with minced onion and salt and pepper to taste. Combine mussel broth with enough water to make 5 cups (1 1/4 L) and add to potato mixture. Simmer until potatoes have fallen apart.

Remove from heat and strain potato mixture through fine sieve.

Return to saucepan and add mussels. Rinse watercress and drain well; discard stems. Add to soup and bring to simmer; simmer 5 to 6 minutes. Remove from heat and stir in crème fraîche, or divide soup among heated bowls and top each serving with a dollop of the crème fraîche.

Mediterranean Fish Soup

Traveling gourmets often find it hard to distinguish among the various fish soups they encounter. Each Mediterranean country (and, of course, every other coastal region in the world) has its own recipe, based on readily available ingredients. But the preparation methods are often very different, as are the various ways in which the soups may be served.

Mediterranean fish soups usually have a consistency midway between soup and stew. They are typically eaten with garlic bread or with a garlic mayonnaise such as the renowned Provençal aïoli.

It is not essential that you use actual Mediterranean fish species, but it *is* critical that the fish be fresh and as small as possible so that a large proportion of heads and bones are included; these make the soup especially flavorful.

4 servings
3 pounds (1400 g) whole fish
For the broth
1 leek
1 carrot
1 stalk celery
1 teaspoon salt
1/2 teaspoon peppercorns

For the soup
1 leek
1 onion
1/2 bulb fresh fennel
3 tablespoons olive oil
1 small chili pepper
1 bay leaf
1 whole clove
1/2 teaspoon salt
A few saffron threads
Grated peel of 1/2 orange
2 cleaned squid (about 7 ounces/200 g each)
10 ounces (200 g) mussels
4 to 6 hard-shelled small clams, such as cherrystones
1 cup (240 mL) white wine

Clean and gut the fish (see page 20); rinse thoroughly. Trim away heads, tails, and fins and cut fish into bite-size pieces. Cover and refrigerate.

Soak trimmings in cold water about 15 minutes. Place in large saucepan and cover with water. Clean and coarsely chop leek, carrot, and celery; add to pan with salt and peppercorns. Bring to simmer, then let mixture simmer gently for 20 to 30 minutes. Strain broth.

Clean and slice remaining leek. Peel and dice onion; coarsely chop fennel. Heat olive oil in large Dutch oven. Add leek, onion, and fennel and sauté 4 to 5 minutes, stirring.

Seed and finely chop chili pepper; add to vegetables with bay leaf, clove, salt, saffron, and orange peel. Stir through and remove from heat.

Rinse squid and peel off skin if desired. Slice bodies into rings. Scrub and debeard mussels. Add squid to vegetables and pour in fish broth. Simmer 4 to 5 minutes, then add mussels and clams, reduce heat, cover, and cook 2 to 3 minutes longer. Add fish pieces and wine; if necessary, add water so that fish is covered with liquid. Cook uncovered over low heat for 8 to 10 minutes, then cover and let stand on turned-off burner another 5 to 6 minutes for flavors to blend.

POACHED AND STEAMED

Lake Trout au Bleu

The liquid used for poaching fish must never be allowed to come to a simmer; in fact, the process might better be called "steeping," since the water should not even show any discernible bubbles. Various poaching liquids can be used depending on the type of fish. The simplest is salted water, but if you wish to heighten the flavor of the fish, a better poaching medium is the flavored broth known as *court bouillon*. And for the finest dish of all, particularly if you are using a choice variety of fish, use stock prepared according to the recipe on page 9.

If you would like the fish to retain the blue color that gives this dish its name, be sure the fish you select has the natural slippery coating over its skin left intact. Be careful not to disturb this coating or to wash it off.

If you want to poach a large whole fish, such as a lake trout, you will need a fish poacher like that pictured on the following page. If you often prepare such fish dishes it is a great piece of equipment to have, as you can cook the fish without in the least damaging its appearance. A fish poacher has a flat perforated insert on which the fish rests and with which it is easily lifted out after cooking.

The classic accompaniments for trout poached *au bleu* are parsleyed potatoes and tender vegetables such as peas, carrots, or zucchini.

4 servings
1 cleaned whole lake trout (about 2¹/₂ pounds/1200 g)
For the poaching liquid
6 cups (1¹/₂ L) water
1 cup (240 mL) dry white wine
2 stalks celery
1 medium carrot
1 large leek
1 small onion
2 teaspoons salt
¹/₂ teaspoon peppercorns
2 bay leaves
1 sprig parsley
1 sprig thyme

First prepare poaching liquid. Combine water and wine in large saucepan. Clean celery, carrot, and leek and cut into coarse strips; peel and quarter onion. Add vegetables to wine mixture. Season with salt, peppercorns, bay leaves, parsley, and thyme. Simmer this *court bouillon* very gently for about 30 minutes.

Thoroughly rinse out cavity of fish. Place on poaching rack and lower into fish poacher. Strain lukewarm *court bouillon*

over fish (or if preferred, vegetables and herbs may be left in broth). Cover poacher and heat just until surface of liquid begins to shake; do not let water reach a simmer. Reduce heat to maintain liquid below the simmering point. Cooking time will depend on size and thickness of fish; allow 10 minutes for every 1¹/₄ inches (3 cm) of thickness. (A 3-inch- or 7.5-cm-thick trout will cook through in 25 minutes.)

Tip: With smaller fish, such as brook or rainbow trout, a special poacher is not necessary. Simply lay the fish in a large pot or Dutch oven, or truss them into curves. To do this, thread a thick needle with heavy-duty cotton thread; draw the thread through the gills and then through the tail of the fish, and knot the ends so that the fish bends into an arc.

Trout Quenelles with Fresh Spinach

A quenelle mixture like this one can be used in many ways—for example, as a stuffing for whole fish (as in the recipe for Stuffed Pike on the following page) or in a terrine.

4 servings
7 ounces (200 g) fresh trout fillets (from 2 trout)
1 egg
Salt and freshly ground pepper
2 scant tablespoons (25 g) butter, softened
1/2 cup (125 mL) whipping or heavy cream, chilled
For the spinach
10 ounces (300 g) fresh spinach
2 tablespoons (30 g) butter
Salt and freshly ground pepper
Freshly grated nutmeg
For the sauce
2 cups (450 mL) fish stock (see recipe, page 9)
1/2 cup (125 mL) white wine
A few saffron threads
1/4 cup (60 mL) whipping or heavy cream, beaten to form stiff peaks
Salt and freshly ground pepper (optional)

Photo 1: Cut trout fillets into pieces and combine in mixing bowl with egg, 1/2 teaspoon salt, and pepper to taste. Cover and chill thoroughly.

Photo 2: Place chilled trout mixture in blender. Add softened butter, cut into small pieces, and pour in cold whipping cream. Blend until smooth, working as quickly as possible to avoid warming the mixture; should it become too warm it will have to be rechilled before it is shaped.

Photo 3: Place a rounded tablespoon of well-chilled trout mixture in the palm of your hand and shape into a smooth oval. Repeat with remaining mixture, arranging quenelles on oiled plate or baking sheet.

Photo 4: Bring a generous amount of salted water to boil in large saucepan. Place each quenelle in the water with a large spoon; use a second spoon to slip the quenelle free. Simmer gently for about 10 minutes.

Photo 5: Pick over spinach, cutting away tough stems; wash leaves thoroughly. Plunge leaves into large pot of rapidly boiling water, then immediately drain and rinse under cold water to stop cooking process. Drain well and pat spinach dry. Heat butter in saucepan until foamy. Add spinach and season with salt, pepper, and nutmeg. Cook briefly over high heat, stirring frequently. Divide spinach among 4 plates and arrange trout quenelles on top.

For the sauce, combine fish stock with white wine and saffron threads in saucepan and bring to boil. Cook, uncovered, until reduced to about 1 cup (240 mL). Fold in whipped cream and, if necessary, season with salt and pepper. Spoon sauce over quenelles and serve.

Pike Quenelles

Not illustrated

4 servings
8 ounces (250 g) pike fillets
1 egg
1 egg yolk
1/2 teaspoon salt
Freshly ground pepper
1 tablespoon chopped fresh parsley
1 slice firm white bread
1/2 cup (125 mL) whipping or heavy cream

This preparation is nearly identical to that of trout quenelles. As in the previous recipe, have the ingredients thoroughly chilled. Trim crust from bread, cut bread into small cubes and soak in the cream to soften. Add softened bread and parsley to blender with remaining ingredients. Form and cook as in the recipe for trout quenelles; serve with spinach and sauce.

Stuffed Pike

If you purchase the fish for this, ask the fish man to open it from the back or the belly and to remove the backbone and all smaller bones.

If you have caught the fish yourself, here's how to prepare it: First, skin the pike by scraping from the tail toward the head using the dull side of a knife. Rinse the fish well under running water. Cut open the belly from head to tail and remove the entrails, then trim away the fins.

To bone the pike, first lift out the top layer of bones through the opening with a sharp knife. Next, work your thumbs through the remaining bones, loosening them, until you reach the backbone. With a sharp knife, loosen the flesh over the backbone, being careful not to cut through the back of the fish. Finally, cut through the backbone at head and tail with kitchen shears and remove it.

4 servings
1 cleaned whole 2-pound (1-kg) pike (1 pound 14 ounces/900 g boned)
Salt
3 ounces (100 g) fresh spinach
7 ounces (200 g) unsmoked bacon (or blanched smoked bacon), very thinly sliced
2 small carrots
1/2 large celery root
1 large leek
2 tablespoons vegetable oil
1 cup (240 mL) dry white wine
For the filling
3 ounces (100 g) fresh trout fillet
1/2 egg
salt and freshly ground pepper
1 tablespoon (15 g) butter
1/4 cup (60 mL) crème fraîche
2 teaspoons chopped fresh dill
For the sauce
1 shallot
1 yellow bell pepper
1 tablespoon (15 g) butter
1 whole clove
A few peppercorns
1 tablespoon dry vermouth
1/2 cup (125 mL) fish stock (see recipe, page 9)
2 tablespoons stiffly whipped cream
Salt

Briefly rinse fish under running water and pat dry inside and out with paper towels. Pick over spinach and wash thoroughly; blanch briefly in boiling salted water. Open the fish and line the inside completely with spinach leaves.

For the filling, blend trout fillet with egg, salt, pepper, butter, and crème fraîche as for the trout quenelles on page 19, adding the dill. Spread atop spinach layer. Close fish and wrap with bacon slices, tying with cotton thread to secure.

Clean carrots, celery root, and leek and chop coarsely. Heat oil in large saucepan or fish poacher. Add vegetables and lay fish on top. Pour in white wine and place in preheated 350°F (180°C) oven. After 30 minutes, turn off oven; let fish rest in oven another 10 to 15 minutes. Remove fish and discard bacon. Cut fish into slices.

While the fish cooks, prepare sauce: Peel and mince shallot. Wash and seed bell pepper, pat dry, and dice finely. Melt butter in saucepan, add shallot, and sauté until translucent. Add pepper cubes, clove, peppercorns, vermouth, and fish stock. Cook until vegetables are very soft, then force mixture through fine sieve. Fold in whipped cream and season with salt. Serve sauce with the stuffed pike.

Sole Fillets with Sherry

Fillets of saltwater fish take on superb flavor when steamed with herbs. With fine ingredients—here including fortified wine, a hint of garlic, and some butter—a great fillet of fish becomes even better. When steamed Chinese style, as in this recipe, the fish cooks in its own juices on a plate or platter fitted into a large pot. It is important to leave enough room between the edge of the plate and the sides of the pot to allow steam to circulate freely. The plate must be set high enough (preferably on a heatproof bowl) that it does not touch the surface of the water, which should be $3/4$ to $1\,1/4$ inches (2 to 3 cm) deep.

2 servings
2 large sole (about 12 ounces/ 375 g each)
Fresh lemon juice (optional)
$1/4$ teaspoon freshly ground white pepper
2 onions
2 tablespoons snipped fresh chives
2 tablespoons finely chopped fresh parsley
$1/2$ cup (125 mL) dry Sherry
$1/2$ cup (125 mL) water
$1/2$ teaspoon salt
3 tablespoons (45 g) butter

Cut off fish heads with kitchen shears. Cut diagonally through dark skin at tail end with sharp knife; loosen skin enough so that fish can be grasped firmly at tail.

Photo 1: Beginning at head end, loosen dark skin at fins with your thumbs to make skinning easier.

Photo 2: Grasp tail firmly and pull dark skin toward head with strong jerking motions. Turn fish over and remove white skin in the same way.

Photo 3: Hold fins up and away from body and trim off with shears.

Photo 4: Insert a flexible knife into the fish so that it lies flat against the bones. Working from head to tail, slide knife deeper and deeper until fillets are cut away. Rinse fillets under cold running water and pat thoroughly dry. Rub with lemon juice, if desired, and with pepper. Cover and refrigerate 1 hour.

Peel onions and slice as thinly as possible. Arrange slices on a large plate or platter that will fit into steaming pot. Pat fillets dry once more and lay on onions skinned side down. Sprinkle with herbs.

Photo 5: Pour Sherry and water into steaming pot and invert small heatproof bowl in center. Cover and bring to boil over medium heat.

Photo 6: Sprinkle fish fillets with salt immediately before placing them in pot. Set plate on top of inverted bowl in steaming pot and cover pot tightly. The fillets will be fully cooked in 5 to 6 minutes.

Lift plate from steamer with two roasting forks, or protect hands with mitts; keep fish warm. If desired, boil down steaming liquid until reduced to a few tablespoons. Add juices from plate and whisk in butter. Serve this light sauce as an accompaniment to sole fillets.

Mixed Fish in Cream Sauce

Fine fish such as porgy, bream, bass, and sole are wonderful when given this delicate treatment. The dish is particularly good served with buttered noodles.

4 servings
1 bass or snapper (13 ounces/300 to 400 g)
2 porgy or bream (8 to 10 ounces/250 to 300 g each)
1 sole (13 ounces/400 g)
8 jumbo shrimp
2 tablespoons (30 g) butter
Salt and freshly ground pepper
1 cup (240 mL) dry white wine
2 teaspoons fresh lime juice
For the stock
1 large leek
2 small carrots
1 stalk celery
1 teaspoon salt
1 teaspoon peppercorns
1 bunch Italian parsley
1 cup (240 mL) dry white wine
For the sauce
1 cup (240 mL) whipping or heavy cream
2 teaspoons dry vermouth
1 teaspoon fresh lime juice
Salt and freshly ground pepper (optional)
Fresh chervil leaves

Scale and fillet the first two fish as described on page 62, but do not skin. Fillet the sole as on page 23. Remove tails from shrimp and devein. Blanch shrimp for a few moments in boiling salted water, then cool and peel.

Using ingredients above, prepare a stock from the fish trimmings (heads, bones, and fins) as described on page 9. Strain through a fine sieve and cook down uncovered until reduced to about 1/2 cup (125 mL). Butter a gratin or other heatproof dish that will fit into the fish poacher. Cut bass and porgy pieces into portion-size chunks; roll up sole fillets. Arrange fish and shrimp in prepared dish; sprinkle with salt, pepper, wine, and lime juice. Place in fish poacher (see page 23) and steam for 8 to 9 minutes. Remove dish from poacher and drain off accumulated juices into reduced fish stock; keep fish warm. Simmer fish stock for a few minutes, then whisk in cream. Flavor with vermouth and lime juice, and season with salt and pepper if necessary. Serve fish with sauce and sprinkle with chervil.

Turbot with Crème Fraîche

Not illustrated

4 servings
4 turbot or halibut fillets (5 to 7 ounces/150 to 200 g each)
Salt and freshly ground pepper
2 medium carrots
1 stalk celery
1 small kohlrabi
2/3 cup (5 ounces/150 g) crème fraîche
2 teaspoons lime juice
1 teaspoon chopped fresh tarragon

Rinse fillets under cold running water and pat dry. Season with salt and pepper. Butter a heatproof dish that will fit in fish poacher. Clean and trim vegetables and cut into fine strips. Place in prepared dish and steam as described on page 23 for 5 to 6 minutes or until very soft. Arrange fillets on top of vegetables and steam 5 to 6 minutes.

Meanwhile, whisk crème fraîche with lime juice and tarragon. Pour over fish and steam 6 to 8 minutes longer.

Steamed Flounder Fillets in Aspic

Fish *en gelée* is superb when it is handled carefully, so that it retains its full flavor, and when a good fish stock is used to make the aspic. If you buy whole fish you will have enough trimmings to make the stock; if you use fillets, have some stock on hand in the freezer.

4 servings

4 flounder (10 ounces/300 g each)
1 small onion
Salt
1 small zucchini
1 large carrot
3/4 cup shelled peas, fresh or frozen
4 ounces (120 g) cooked, peeled shrimp
4 ounces (120 g) mussels
Grated peel of 1/2 lemon

For the stock

1/2 onion
1 medium carrot
1 parsley root
1 leek
1/2 large celery root
Salt
4 to 6 cups (1 to 1 1/2 L) water

For the aspic

2 envelopes unflavored gelatin
1/2 cup cold water
6 tablespoons (75 mL) dry white wine
Salt and freshly ground pepper

Using sharp knife, cut off heads of flounder; trim away fins with kitchen shears. Lay fish on work surface and cut through skin diagonally at tail with sharp knife. Starting at this cut, use knife to loosen skin enough that it can be easily grasped. Press fish tail down with your left hand and pull away skin with your right, using a paper towel for better grip. Repeat on other side, then cut fillets away from bones.

Combine all fish trimmings in large saucepan. Trim and finely dice onion, carrot, parsley root, leek, and celery root and add to pan. Sprinkle with salt and pour in water. Simmer stock gently for 1 hour, then strain through fine sieve.

For steaming, oil a platter or plate that will fit into a large covered pot. Peel onion and slice as thinly as possible. Arrange a layer of onion slices on plate and cover with fish fillets. Season with salt. Pour water into pot, invert small heatproof bowl in center and set plate of fish on top; water should not touch bottom of plate. Cover pot and bring to simmer, then steam 5 to 6 minutes. Remove plate and let fish cool. Meanwhile, simmer fish stock uncovered until reduced to about 3 cups (700 mL).

Scrub zucchini under running water and trim ends; slice thinly. Trim carrot and cut into fine julienne. Boil zucchini, carrot, and peas in small amount of salted water until crisp-tender, 5 to 6 minutes. Divide vegetables, shrimp, mussels, and steamed fish among four soup plates and sprinkle with grated lemon peel. Soften gelatin in cold water. Add to fish stock and warm gently until gelatin is completely dissolved. Stir in wine and cool almost to room temperature. Divide among the soup plates and chill until firm, 1 to 2 hours.

FROM THE SKILLET

Sautéed Whitefish Amandine

Fish can also be sautéed without an initial flour coating; fine freshwater types such as whitefish and brook trout are especially good this way. Parsleyed potatoes and, in season, fresh asparagus are perfect side dishes.

2 servings
2 cleaned whole whitefish (10 ounces/300 g each)
Salt
Juice of 1/2 lemon
2 sprigs tarragon
2 sprigs parsley
3 tablespoons (50 g) butter
1/2 cup (50 g) sliced almonds

If cleaned whitefish are not available at the fish market, purchase whole whitefish and gut and scale them (see page 20); trim away the fins with kitchen shears.

Rinse fish briefly under running water and pat dry. Sprinkle a little salt inside body cavity and squeeze in a few drops of lemon juice. Insert 1 sprig of each of the herbs into each fish and close the opening with a wooden skewer to prevent the cut from curving open during cooking.

Melt half the butter in a large skillet and add almonds. After about 1 minute add fish and cook on both sides over gentle heat to prevent butter from darkening. The skin may loosen somewhat, but this will not do any harm—just the opposite, in fact, since the butter will flavor the fish. Add remaining butter before turning the fish. Total cooking time will be about 10 to 12 minutes.

Transfer fish to heated plates, sprinkle with almonds and pour browned butter over.

Salmon Steaks with Mushrooms

Not illustrated

4 servings
7 ounces (200 g) mushrooms
2 tablespoons vegetable oil
2 tablespoons finely chopped shallot
2 tablespoons chopped fresh parsley
Salt
4 salmon steaks (4 ounces/120 g each)
Freshly ground pepper
3 tablespoons (40 g) butter

Trim mushrooms and slice very thinly. Heat oil in large skillet. Add shallot and sauté until translucent. Add mushroom slices, parsley, and 1/2 teaspoon salt; cook over medium-high heat, stirring constantly, 2 to 3 minutes. Remove from heat and keep warm. Lightly salt and pepper salmon steaks. Melt butter in another skillet and add salmon. Cook over medium heat (to keep butter from burning) for 2 to 3 minutes on one side, then turn. Spoon mushroom mixture over fish and cook 5 minutes more over medium heat. Serve on heated plates.

Swordfish Sicilian Style

Because they are so firm and meaty, swordfish and tuna steaks lend themselves particularly well to skillet cooking. This recipe is also excellent with halibut, haddock, or cod, however, as these fish taste delicious with Mediterranean seasonings. Serve crusty Italian bread, along with a vegetable such as broccoli, zucchini, or eggplant.

4 servings
1 large onion
1/2 bay leaf, crumbled
1/2 clove garlic, crushed
Freshly ground pepper
1/2 teaspoon salt
4 swordfish steaks (7 ounces/200 g each)
1/2 cup (125 mL) olive oil
1 tablespoon dried oregano
Lemon slices

Peel and thinly slice onion; combine with crumbled bay leaf, crushed garlic, pepper to taste, and the salt. Place 1 swordfish steak in a large bowl and scatter with some of onion mixture. Top with second piece of fish; continue alternating layers until all ingredients are used. Pour olive oil over all. Cover with foil and let marinate 3 to 4 hours.

Remove swordfish from marinade and wipe off onion mixture. Sprinkle both sides of steaks with oregano. Strain olive oil into large skillet and place over medium-high heat. Add fish and cook until golden brown, 3 to 4 minutes on each side. Serve with lemon slices.

Perch Fillets with Lemon and Capers

Not illustrated

4 servings
4 perch fillets (7 ounces/200 g each)
1 tablespoon flour
1/2 large onion
1 medium carrot
1 large stalk celery
4 tablespoons (60 mL) olive oil
1 teaspoon salt
2 tablespoons finely chopped fresh basil
2 lemons
2 tablespoons capers

Pat fillets thoroughly dry with paper towels and coat very lightly on both sides with flour. Trim onion, carrot, and celery and dice finely.

Heat 2 tablespoons olive oil in large skillet, add vegetables, and sauté 3 to 4 minutes over medium heat. Season with salt and basil and immediately remove from heat. Transfer mixture to bowl.

Heat remaining 2 tablespoons olive oil in same skillet, add fish, and cook until golden brown, 3 to 4 minutes per side. Divide vegetable mixture atop fillets. Peel lemons, removing all white pith, and cut into very thin slices. Garnish fish with lemon slices and sprinkle with capers. Return to heat briefly to warm through, then serve immediately.

Sole Meunière

The phrase *à la meunière* simply signifies "coated with flour" — since the word *meunière* means miller's wife. Fish prepared in this way becomes golden and crusty when fried, while the flesh stays tender and moist.

Flatfish such as sole, flounder, and fluke are perfectly suited to cooking *à la meunière* because the thin fillets are well protected by their flour coating. But many other types, from either fresh or salt water, also lend themselves well to this treatment — both small, portion-size fish and fillets of larger fish, which might dry out during cooking without the thin coating of flour.

The classic accompaniment for *Sole Meunière* is plain boiled or parsleyed potatoes.

1 serving
1 cleaned whole sole (10 to 12 ounces/300 to 350 g)
Salt
Flour
2 tablespoons vegetable oil
2 tablespoons (30 g) butter
For garnish
1 lemon wedge
1 sprig parsley

Rinse fish briefly under cold running water. To remove dark skin, place fish on work surface dark skin up and cut diagonally through skin at tail using sharp knife. Loosen skin with knife far enough that you can get a firm grip on it. Hold down tail with left hand and, using a paper towel for better grip, pull off skin with right hand. Cut off the fish head. Sprinkle fish with salt and coat lightly with flour on both sides, pressing flour in well. (If fish is too dry for flour to adhere well, moisten surface with water before flouring.) Set fish aside on rack for a few minutes to let flour coating dry slightly.

Heat oil in skillet, add sole skinned side down, and cook over high heat 2 to 3 minutes. Melt butter in small saucepan. Turn fish, at the same time pouring off oil. Add melted butter to skillet, reduce heat, and cook until fish is done; the butter should brown lightly without burning. Serve fish with lemon wedge and garnish with parsley.

Tip: During cooking, take care to keep the flesh of the fish as moist as possible. With either small individual fish or thin fillets such as sole, this is best accomplished over high heat. Thick fillets or large fish should be started over high heat until they form a crust; then the heat is reduced until the interior cooks through. For high-temperature cooking use vegetable oil or clarified butter, since regular butter will burn. But because the taste of whole butter is a perfect complement to the mild fish, a luxurious compromise is to begin cooking the fish in oil, then to pour off the oil and finish with butter.

Herbed Salmon Sauté

Prepare this recipe only when you can get really fresh salmon and shrimp. Serve with a crisp vegetable such as snow peas.

4 servings
4 salmon steaks (7 ounces/200 g each)
Salt and freshly ground pepper
Flour
4 large shrimp
2 tablespoons vegetable oil
2 tablespoons (30 g) butter
1/2 clove garlic
2 tablespoons minced shallot
2 tablespoons chopped fresh herbs (parsley, thyme, basil, dill, tarragon, and lovage or celery leaves)
1/2 cup (125 mL) dry white wine

Lightly season both sides of salmon steaks with salt and pepper, then coat both sides lightly with flour. Pull tails off shrimp and split shells lengthwise with serrated knife. This will expose the dark vein on each shrimp. Remove vein and halve shrimp lengthwise.

Heat oil in skillet. Add salmon steaks and cook over medium heat about 4 minutes on one side. Add butter to pan, turn steaks, and add shrimp, cut sides down. Cook 4 to 5 minutes, then remove fish and shrimp and keep warm.

Peel and crush garlic. Add to skillet with shallot and sauté briefly. Add herbs and wine, increase heat to high, and boil until sauce is reduced by half. Return fish and shrimp to skillet and warm through, then serve immediately.

Flounder Hamburg Style

A traditional German recipe characterized by the addition of bacon. Serve with boiled potatoes. Not illustrated.

4 servings
4 dressed flounder, fluke, or plaice (10 to 13 ounces/300 to 400 g each)
Juice of 1 lemon
4 ounces (120 g) bacon
Salt
Flour
Lemon slices and fresh parsley

Remove head, tail, and fins from fish. Rinse fish under running water, pat dry, and sprinkle with lemon juice.

Finely dice bacon and cook in large skillet until fat is rendered. Remove bacon pieces and set aside. Season fish with salt and coat with flour. Add to bacon fat in skillet and cook over high heat 4 to 5 minutes per side. Divide among heated plates and sprinkle with bacon bits. Garnish with lemon slices and parsley.

Pollock Roulades with Leek

Excellent roulades can also be made with other fish fillets—for example, perch or cod.

4 servings
6 to 8 thin pollock fillets (about 1 to 1¼ pounds/500 to 600 g)
6 to 8 very thin bacon slices
1 tablespoon vegetable oil
¼ cup (60 mL) fish or meat stock
For the stuffing
1 tablespoon fresh lemon juice
½ teaspoon salt
Freshly ground pepper
1 teaspoon chopped fresh sage
1½ teaspoons medium-sharp mustard
1 large leek
1 tablespoon vegetable oil

Thin fillets are the best choice for fish roulades. If you can only get thick ones, split them in half horizontally.

Spread out fillets on work surface and sprinkle with lemon juice, then with salt, pepper, and sage. Thinly spread half of each fillet with mustard. Clean and mince leek. Heat 1 tablespoon oil in small skillet, add leek, and sauté until tender. Divide among fillets. Roll up fillets from one end and wrap each with a bacon slice. Secure ends with toothpicks.

Heat remaining 1 tablespoon oil in skillet over very high heat. Add roulades and sauté briefly on all sides. Reduce heat, pour in stock, and cook gently, turning frequently, for 10 to 12 minutes; liquid should evaporate completely.

Shrimp-stuffed Cod Roulades

A piquant tomato sauce makes a good accompaniment. Not illustrated.

4 servings
4 cod fillets (5 to 7 ounces/150 to 200 g each)
Salt and freshly ground pepper
3 tablespoons vegetable oil
½ cup (125 mL) fish or chicken stock
For the stuffing
4 tablespoons (60 mL) vegetable oil
2 tablespoons minced onion
1 tablespoon capers
2 anchovy fillets
1 tablespoon chopped fresh parsley
Salt and freshly ground pepper
4 ounces (120 g) cooked, peeled shrimp
½ cup (125 mL) dry white wine

Briefly rinse cod fillets under cold running water and pat dry with paper towels. Spread out on work surface and season with salt and pepper.

For the stuffing, heat 1 tablespoon oil in skillet, add onion, and sauté until tender. Coarsely chop capers and anchovies and stir into onion with parsley. Season with salt and pepper. Chop shrimp and add to onion mixture. Pour in wine and cook uncovered over high heat for 3 to 4 minutes or until liquid is nearly evaporated. Divide warm stuffing mixture among cod fillets. Roll up and secure with cotton thread or wooden skewers.

Heat 3 tablespoons oil in skillet. Add roulades and sauté on all sides over medium-high heat. Pour in stock and cook over medium heat 10 to 12 minutes longer.

Cod Fillets with Asparagus and Sorrel Sauce

4 servings

1 generous pound (500 g) asparagus
Salt
4 cod fillets (5 to 7 ounces/150 to 200 g each)
Freshly ground pepper
2 tablespoons vegetable oil
3 tablespoons (50 g) butter
For the sauce
2 cups (450 mL) fish stock
1/2 cup (125 mL) dry white wine
Salt and freshly ground pepper
1 cup (60 g) sorrel
7 tablespoons (100 g) butter, chilled
6 tablespoons whipped cream
1 lime or lemon

Start by preparing the sauce, as the reduction takes some time. Simmer fish stock over medium heat until reduced to about 1 cup (240 mL). Add white wine, season with salt and pepper, and reduce to 1 generous cup (240 mL); keep warm. While stock mixture is reducing, prepare asparagus and fish fillets. Trim and wash asparagus; tie into bundles. Bring a large amount of salted water to boil, add asparagus, and cook to desired tenderness, about 20 to 30 minutes.

Pat fish dry with paper towels and season lightly with salt and pepper. Heat oil in large skillet, add fish, and cook on one side over high heat for 3 minutes. Turn fish and pour off oil; cut butter into small pieces and distribute over fish. Reduce heat to low and cook fish another 4 minutes, turning once if necessary. Keep warm.

Cut sorrel into narrow strips. Return stock mixture to simmer, add sorrel, and simmer 1 to 2 minutes. Cut chilled butter into small pieces and whisk into sorrel mixture; sauce should be creamy, not runny. Fold in whipped cream. Divide fish, asparagus, and sauce among 4 plates and garnish with lime or lemon slices.

Fish Fillets with Curry Sauce

Not illustrated

4 servings

4 cod, haddock, or perch fillets (7 ounces/200 g each)
Salt
3 tablespoons vegetable oil
1/2 red bell pepper
1/2 green bell pepper
1 small chili pepper
1 tablespoon chopped onion
1 cup (240 mL) dry white wine
Juice of 1 lime
1 tablespoon curry powder
1 banana, sliced
2 tablespoons breadcrumbs
2 tablespoons (30 g) butter

Rinse fish fillets under cold running water and pat dry.

Season lightly with salt. Heat oil in large skillet. Add fillets and cook on one side until golden, about 4 minutes. Remove from skillet and keep warm.

Meanwhile, seed and mince bell peppers and chili pepper. Add peppers and onion to skillet in which fish was cooked and sauté until tender. Stir in wine, lime juice, curry powder, salt, and sliced banana. Simmer until banana is falling apart, 5 to 6 minutes.

Arrange fish fillets atop sauce cooked side down. Sprinkle with breadcrumbs and dot with butter. Place under preheated broiler until top is lightly browned, 4 to 6 minutes. Serve immediately.

Pan-Fried Porgy

Fried single-serving-size fish are a special treat. Many kinds of fish lend themselves to this cooking method—porgy, redfish, bream, flatfish such as flounder and sole, and freshwater fish like trout, perch, and whitefish. The coating of flour, egg, and breadcrumbs (or cornmeal, or ground almonds) protects the flesh, keeping it flavorful and moist. Fish coated with such a breading can also be deep-fried (see page 86); in fact, deep frying is even easier than pan frying, because you must take special care in pan frying not to damage or loosen the crumb coating. But for those who do not own a deep fryer or who don't want to use such a large quantity of oil, pan frying is the ideal solution. The result is not always as handsome as with deep frying because the breading does not become as uniformly golden brown, but the flavor of pan-fried fish cannot be better.

Pan-fried fish can be served with a wide variety of side dishes. Potato salad made with vinaigrette is particularly good, as are parsleyed potatoes. For an even simpler menu, just serve the fish with French or Italian bread.

4 servings
4 whole porgy (10 to 13 ounces/300 to 400 g each)
Salt and freshly ground pepper
4 very thin lemon slices
Fresh parsley
1 tablespoon capers
For breading
Flour
1 egg, beaten
Breadcrumbs
For frying
6 tablespoons (90 mL) vegetable oil
1/4 cup (60 g) butter

Scale fish and remove entrails (see page 20). Trim away fins with kitchen shears. Rinse fish thoroughly under running water and pat dry inside and out with paper towels. Season with salt and pepper. Cut away peel from lemon slices; place 1 slice inside each fish along with some parsley and capers. Secure opening with cotton thread. Dredge fish in flour, dip in beaten egg, and then coat with breadcrumbs, pressing them in well.

Heat oil in large skillet over medium heat. Place fish in skillet and fry 2 minutes on each side. Pour off oil and dot fish with butter. Reduce heat to low and cook 4 to 5 minutes longer on both sides.

Tip: Using first oil and then butter may seem needlessly complicated, but there are good reasons for this method. The first cooking in oil firms up the breading and helps it brown uniformly; the slow final cooking in butter gives the fish excellent flavor that cannot be duplicated with oil.

Carp Alsatian Style

Fish and sauerkraut may seem an odd combination, but this original dish is delicious. Because it has a lot of flavor, carp is especially good here. Serve with parsleyed potatoes and cold beer.

4 servings
1 whole cleaned carp (2¹/₂ pounds/1200 g)
Salt
Flour
1 egg, beaten
1 cup (100 g) breadcrumbs
6 tablespoons (75 mL) vegetable oil
3 tablespoons (50 g) butter
lemon wedges
For the stock
1 medium carrot
¹/₂ large celery root
¹/₂ onion
1 parsley root
¹/₂ bay leaf
¹/₂ teaspoon salt
A few peppercorns
For the sauerkraut
¹/₂ small onion
2 ounces (50 g) bacon
1 generous pound (500 g) sauerkraut
¹/₂ cup (125 mL) dry white wine
4 to 5 juniper berries
1 bay leaf
Salt (optional)
For the sauce
2 cups (450 mL) fish stock (made with carp trimmings)
1¹/₂ teaspoons chopped fresh tarragon
¹/₂ cup (125 mL) whipping or heavy cream
Salt and freshly ground pepper

Thoroughly rinse inside of fish under running water. Remove scales by scraping fish with dull edge of knife from tail toward head. Cut central part of fish into 4 or 8 uniform steaks (depending on whether you would like each serving to consist of two thinner pieces or one thicker).

For stock, cut fish head in half and place in large saucepan with remaining trimmings. Cover with water. Trim and chop carrot, celery root, onion, and parsley root and add to saucepan with bay leaf, salt, and peppercorns. Bring to simmer; let mixture simmer gently 1 hour. Strain through fine sieve. Return 2 cups (450 mL) stock to clean saucepan and simmer until reduced to ¹/₂ cup (125 mL).

For the sauerkraut, peel and finely chop onion. Dice bacon. Combine onion and bacon in heavy, large saucepan and cook over low heat until translucent. Add sauerkraut, white wine, juniper berries, and bay leaf; season with salt if necessary. Simmer sauerkraut for 15 to 20 minutes.

Lightly salt carp pieces. Dredge in flour, dip into beaten egg, and then coat with breadcrumbs, pressing to help them adhere. Heat oil in large skillet and add fish. Cook over medium-high heat for 2 minutes on one side, then turn and cook second side for 2 minutes. Pour off oil and dot fish with the butter (this will give the dish better flavor). Cook carp in butter another 3 to 4 minutes on both sides. For sauce, bring reduced stock to a simmer, then remove from heat and add tarragon; let steep for 3 to 4 minutes. Whip cream to soft peaks and whisk into stock. Season with salt and pepper.

Serve fried carp with sauerkraut and with lemon wedges, if desired. Accompany with the delicate tarragon sauce.

FROM THE OVEN

Baked Burgundy Carp

The secret to perfect results with baked fish is cooking it in the right amount of fat or liquid. For this recipe try to get a fish that has been held in a tank of fresh water for a few days to flush away its "mossy" taste. Serve with French bread toasted with garlic-herb butter.

4 servings
1 whole cleaned carp (about 2¹/₂ pounds/1200 g)
1 large shallot
3 tablespoons vegetable oil
1 small zucchini
Salt and freshly ground pepper
³/₄ cup breadcrumbs
3 tablespoons (50 g) butter
For the marinade
¹/₂ teaspoon salt
Freshly ground pepper
¹/₂ bay leaf
¹/₂ teaspoon dried thyme
Juice of ¹/₂ lemon
1¹/₂ cups (350 mL) red Burgundy

Scale carp if desired; wash thoroughly under running water. (Since the carp is going to be breaded and not prepared *au bleu*, it doesn't matter if the slippery coating on its skin is washed away.) Cut fish crosswise into 4 or 5 pieces and place in large bowl. Add salt, pepper, crushed bay leaf, thyme, lemon juice, and wine and coat fish well. Cover and marinate a minimum of 2 to 3 hours.

Peel and mince shallot. Heat oil in flameproof oval baking dish large enough to hold fish. Add shallot and sauté until tender; do not brown. Scrub zucchini and trim ends; slice thinly. Arrange slices in the baking dish and season lightly with salt and pepper. Heat on top of stove until oil begins to bubble. Remove fish from marinade and reassemble in baking dish atop zucchini. Pour marinade over and sprinkle with breadcrumbs. Bake on lowest rack of preheated 425°F (220°C) oven for 10 minutes. Meanwhile, melt butter. Brush fish with some of melted butter and bake another 10 minutes. Brush with remaining butter and bake about 20 more minutes.

Mackerel with Fennel

Not illustrated

4 servings
4 cleaned small mackerel (10 to 13 ounces/300 to 400 g each)
Salt and freshly ground pepper
2 fennel bulbs (about 13 ounces/400 g)
7 ounces (200 g) plum tomatoes
3 tablespoons vegetable oil
1 tablespoon chopped fresh parsley
1 cup (240 mL) dry white wine
3 to 4 tablespoons breadcrumbs
3 tablespoons (40 g) butter

Wash mackerel well under running water and pat dry with paper towels. Season with salt and pepper. Trim fennel bulbs and slice thinly. Blanch tomatoes; peel, seed, and dice.

Heat oil in large skillet, add fennel and tomato, and cook over medium heat 5 to 6 minutes. Sprinkle with parsley and ¹/₂ teaspoon salt. Pour in wine, lay mackerel on top, sprinkle breadcrumbs over, and dot with butter. Bake on middle rack of preheated 400°F (200°C) oven for 25 to 30 minutes.

Stuffed Fish Provençale

Photo, front

1 serving

1 whole trout, porgy, or other fish (1 pound/450 g; about 12 ounces/350 g cleaned)

Salt and freshly ground pepper

2 to 3 tablespoons olive oil

1/2 clove garlic, crushed

1 tablespoon finely chopped onion

1 teaspoon chopped fresh sage

A few chopped fresh rosemary leaves

1 teaspoon chopped fresh parsley

1/2 teaspoon grated lemon peel

3 to 4 black olives

For the stuffing

1 slice white bread without crust

1/4 cup (60 mL) milk

1 teaspoon chopped fresh parsley

1 tablespoon finely chopped onion

Pinch of salt

Freshly ground pepper

Slit open belly of fish with a sharp knife and remove entrails. Scale fish (see page 20), wash well, and pat dry with paper towels. Cut parallel slits into outside of fish about 1/3 inch (1 cm) apart to help fish cook more quickly and evenly and to let fla-vor of seasonings penetrate. Season lightly with salt and pep-per.

For the stuffing, soften bread in milk and squeeze dry. Com-bine in bowl with 1 tablespoon each parsley and onion; season with salt and pepper and mix well. Sprinkle inside of fish with salt and spoon in stuffing. Secure opening with white cot-ton thread.

Heat oil in flameproof oval baking dish large enough to hold fish. Add crushed garlic and chopped onion. Place fish in baking dish and cook on one side over high heat for 1 minute. Turn fish and sprinkle with chopped herbs, lemon peel, and olives. Place on middle rack of preheated 400°F (200°C) oven and bake 20 minutes.

Fish on a Bed of Vegetables

Photo, rear

1 serving

1 whole fish (1 pound/450 g)

Salt and freshly ground pepper

1/2 medium zucchini

1/2 medium leek

1 stalk celery

1/2 medium carrot

1/4 medium onion

2 tablespoons vegetable oil

1/2 cup (125 mL) dry white wine

2 tablespoons (25 g) butter

Clean, scale, wash, and dry fish as in preceding recipe. Trim away fins with kitchen shears. Lightly season fish inside and out with salt and pepper. Scrub the piece of zucchini under run-ning water and cut into fine julienne. Trim and chop remain-ing vegetables. Peel onion and slice into rings. Heat oil in flame-proof oval baking dish large enough to hold fish. Add onion rings and sauté briefly, then add remaining vegetables. Lay fish on top, pour wine over, and bake on middle rack of pre-heated 400°F (200°C) oven 10 minutes. Dot with butter and bake until cooked through, about 10 minutes longer.

Butterfish
à la Bretonne

Some dishes are best made with very small fish, and just aren't as successful when a larger one is substituted. Such is the case with this recipe. Because small fish are cooked in very little time, the ingredients and techniques used with them are not necessarily the same as for larger fish. Admittedly, the small ones are a bit more work to prepare, but the effort is repaid with exquisite flavor. Try serving this with a crisp green salad and French bread.

4 servings
8 small whole butterfish, porgy, or snapper (3 ounces/100 g each)
Salt and freshly ground pepper
1 bunch parsley
2 tablespoons olive oil
3 tablespoons finely chopped shallot
3 tablespoons breadcrumbs
1 clove garlic
4 anchovy fillets
1¹/₂ teaspoons capers
2 tablespoons tomato paste
2 tablespoons chopped fresh herbs (parsley, thyme, basil, sage, and a little rosemary)
2 tablespoons (30 g) butter

If fish were not cleaned when purchased, remove entrails, scale, (see page 20) and wash carefully under running water. Trim away fins. Pat fish dry with paper towels and lightly sprinkle inside and out with salt and pepper. Place a small sprig of parsley inside each fish.

Heat olive oil in large flame-proof baking dish and sauté chopped shallot until tender. Remove half of shallot, mix with breadcrumbs, and set aside. Peel and crush garlic. Finely chop anchovies; coarsely chop capers. Add tomato paste, garlic, anchovies, capers, herbs, and salt to taste to shallot remaining in dish and cook, stirring, for 2 minutes. Place fish in dish, sprinkle with breadcrumb-shallot mixture and dot with butter. Bake on middle rack of preheated 425°F (220°C) oven for 12 to 15 minutes.

Variation: Mullet with Mussels

This is if anything even more delicious than the master recipe. Use 8 small mullet, butterfish, perch, or other small fish, about 3 ounces (80 to 100 g) each, and 7 ounces (200 g) cooked shelled mussels (to cook mussels see page 12). The remaining ingredients are the same as those in the master recipe.

Clean and prepare fish, then make the sauce. Arrange fish atop sauce (without crumbs) and bake 5 to 6 minutes in preheated oven. Scatter mussels around fish, sprinkle everything with breadcrumb mixture, dot with butter, and bake another 8 to 10 minutes.

Fish Fillets Florentine

4 servings
l generous pound (500 g) fresh spinach
l tablespoon (20 g) butter
3 tablespoons whipping or heavy cream
Salt
$1/4$ teaspoon freshly ground white pepper
Pinch of freshly grated nutmeg
7 ounces (200 g) medium tomatoes
3 green onions
2 cod or other fish fillets (5 to 7 ounces/150 to 200 g each)
Fresh lemon juice
For the sauce
$1^1/2$ tablespoons (20 g) butter
1 tablespoon flour
1 cup (240 mL) lukewarm milk
3 ounces (100 g) semi-aged Gouda cheese
1 egg yolk
Salt

Wash and pick over spinach. Blanch briefly in large pot of boiling water and drain well. Heat butter and cream; add spinach, 1 teaspoon salt, pepper, and nutmeg and mix well.

Spread spinach in buttered flameproof baking dish. Score a cross in stem ends of tomatoes and blanch briefly in boiling water. Peel and slice. Trim green onions, discarding tough green leaves; thinly slice white parts. Scatter tomato and onion slices over spinach. Sprinkle fish with lemon juice and salt; set fillets on bed of vegetables. Cover baking dish with foil and bake on middle rack of preheated 400°F (200°C) oven for 25 minutes.

For sauce, melt butter over low heat. Stir in flour and cook until light golden. Vigorously whisk in milk and simmer for several minutes over low heat. Grate cheese and stir into sauce. Whisk in egg yolk and season with salt.

Spoon sauce over fish and bake uncovered for 10 more minutes.

Tomato Fish

Not illustrated

4 servings
1 small onion
1 clove garlic
2 stalks celery
3 tablespoons (50 g) butter
12 ounces (400 g) tomatoes
$1^1/4$ pounds (600 g) perch or cod fillets
$1/2$ teaspoon salt
Freshly ground pepper
1 teaspoon Hungarian sweet paprika
1 tablespoon chopped fresh parsley

Peel and finely chop onion; peel and crush garlic. Finely chop celery. Melt butter in flameproof baking dish large enough to hold fish. Add onion, garlic, and celery and sauté until tender. Score a cross in stem ends of tomatoes and blanch briefly in boiling water, then peel and slice. Pat fish fillets dry and lay on work surface. Season with salt, pepper, paprika, and parsley. Layer fillets in baking dish and top with tomato slices. Cover with greased parchment paper. Bake on middle rack of preheated 400°F (200°C) oven for 25 to 30 minutes.

Fish en Croûte

Photo on pages 54-55

When fish is baked in crisp, golden pastry crust it not only looks attractive but also retains its flavor and aroma exceptionally well. If it is first filled with a savory stuffing, so much the better!

For such a festive dish you will naturally want to use the best-quality fish you can find. Its tasty flesh makes pike well worth the trouble to prepare, and the sophisticated artichoke stuffing harmonizes particularly well with the flavor of this fish.

The simplest way to prepare the crust is with purchased frozen puff pastry, which bakes to an attractive golden brown in just about the time it takes for the fish to cook through. If you prefer, you may also use an unsweetened short pastry or *pâte brisée*; be sure to roll it out thinly so that it bakes through. Tender young snow peas or sugar snap peas are a perfect accompaniment to this dish.

4 servings
1 whole pike or perch (about 3 pounds/1500 g)
Salt
1 medium bell pepper
1/2 lime or lemon
1 1/4 pounds (600 g) frozen puff pastry
1 egg yolk
1/3 cup (80 g) butter
For the stuffing
1 large shallot
2 tablespoons vegetable oil
4 to 8 fresh artichoke bottoms
2 tablespoons white wine
1 egg yolk
Salt and freshly ground pepper
Grated lemon peel
1 teaspoon chopped fresh parsley
1 teaspoon chopped fresh dill
1/4 cup (125 mL) stiffly whipped cream
Dill sprigs

Slit fish open at belly and remove entrails. Wash well under running water and pat dry with paper towels. Trim away fins from back and sides. Season fish lightly with salt on all sides. Halve and seed bell pepper. Squeeze lime or lemon into pepper halves and let stand a few minutes; the juice will extract flavor from the pepper. Rub inside of fish with the flavored juice.

Thaw puff pastry according to package directions.

For the stuffing, peel and mince shallot. Heat oil in large nonaluminum saucepan and sauté shallot until tender. Coarsely dice artichoke bottoms and add to pan with wine; cook over low heat 5 to 6 minutes. Mash artichoke and force through sieve, or puree in food processor. Transfer to mixing bowl and whisk in egg yolk. Season with salt, pepper, a bit of grated lemon peel, and the herbs and let cook completely. Place bowl of artichoke mixture in a larger bowl of ice cubes and stir vigorously until stuffing is chilled through. Gradually stir in cream.

Stuff fish with artichoke mixture and lay a few dill sprigs over the opening. Roll out puff pastry on floured work surface until double the size of the fish. Lay fish on one half of pastry and brush edges of pastry with lightly beaten egg yolk. Fold over other half of pastry to enclose fish, trimming away and reserving excess. Press edges together firmly to seal. Brush bottom edges of pastry with yolk and press to underside of fish, molding pastry around contours of fish. Set on baking sheet that has been lightly rinsed with water.

Press dough trimmings into a ball and let rest for 5 to 10 minutes, then roll out thinly and cut fins, eyes, and scales. Brush pastry-covered fish with egg yolk. For tail fin, press lines into pastry with back of knife. For scales, cut disks about $5/8$ inch ($1^1/2$ cm) in diameter and layer over fish in a scale pattern, working from tail toward head; this is somewhat time consuming but will greatly enhance its appearance. Form eyes and head from pastry. Cut fins from pastry and attach to fish with egg yolk.

Preheat oven to 425°F (220°C). Bake fish on lowest oven rack until light golden, 5 to 10 minutes. Reduce temperature to 350°F (180°C) and bake 40 minutes longer, covering any areas that brown too quickly with foil or parchment paper.

Slide fish onto serving platter. Heat butter until very lightly browned and serve with fish.

Shrimp-stuffed Sea Bass

Not Illustrated

4 servings

1 whole cleaned sea bass (about 3 pounds/1500 g)
Salt and freshly ground pepper
$1^1/4$ pounds (600 g) frozen puff pastry
1 egg yolk
$1/3$ cup (80 g) butter, melted

For the stuffing

1 slice firm white bread, crusts trimmed
A few drops Cognac
$1/4$ cup (60 mL) dry white wine
1 small shallot
3 ounces (80 g) peeled small shrimp
2 tablespoons (30 g) butter
Salt
1 tablespoon chopped fresh herbs (parsley, tarragon, lemon balm, and dill)

Trim away back and side fins from fish. Rinse fish well under running water and pat dry with paper towels. Season inside with salt and pepper.

For the stuffing, place bread in bowl and sprinkle with Cognac. Pour wine over and let soak. Peel and finely chop shallot or onion. Coarsely chop shrimp. Melt butter in skillet. Add shallot and sauté until tender. Add shrimp and cook until semi-opaque. Tear bread into small pieces and add to skillet with salt and herbs; cook for a few minutes longer. Let cool partially, then stuff into fish.

Proceed as in the previous recipe, using the same baking time. Serve with melted butter.

Stuffed Redfish with Shrimp

This can also be made with other salt or freshwater fish.

4 servings

4 whole cleaned redfish or snapper (10 to 13 ounces/300 to 400 g each)
Salt
4 large tomatoes
2 medium shallots
1 clove garlic
$^{1}/_{2}$ bell pepper
3 tablespoons vegetable oil
7 ounces (200 g) cooked, peeled medium shrimp
1 tablespoon chopped fresh basil

For the stuffing

2 tablespoons (30 g) butter
2 tablespoons chopped shallot or onion
2 cups (150 g) beet greens or fresh spinach leaves
2 tablespoons white wine
Salt and freshly ground pepper

Scale fish and rinse well under running water inside and out. Pat thoroughly dry. Season inside of fish lightly with salt.

For stuffing, melt butter. Add shallot or onion and sauté until tender. Wash and pick over greens; chop coarsely. Add to shallot and cook over medium heat 1 to 2 minutes. Add wine, season with salt and pepper, and cook another 2 to 3 minutes. Stuff fish with vegetable mixture and secure opening with wooden skewers.

Blanch tomatoes briefly in boiling water, then peel, seed, and dice. Peel and chop shallots; peel and crush garlic. Seed and finely chop bell pepper. Heat oil in flameproof baking dish large enough to hold fish. Add shallots, garlic, and pepper and sauté until tender. Lay fish in baking dish and cook on top of stove for 2 minutes. Remove from heat and turn fish. Distribute tomatoes evenly in dish. Bake on middle rack of preheated 400°F (200°C) oven for 15 to 20 minutes, basting occasionally with tomato mixture. Five minutes before end of cooking time, add shrimp and sprinkle fish with basil.

Redfish with Artichokes

Not illustrated

4 servings

4 cleaned whole redfish (10 to 13 ounces/300 to 400 g each)
Salt and freshly ground pepper
12 medium-size fresh artichokes
7 ounces (200 g) tomatoes
1 small onion
$^{1}/_{4}$ cup (60 mL) vegetable oil
$^{1}/_{4}$ cup (60 mL) white wine
$^{1}/_{2}$ cup (125 mL) whipping or heavy cream
2 tablespoons chopped fresh herbs (dill, parsley, thyme, and basil)

Prepare redfish as in preceding recipe, then season lightly with salt and pepper.

Trim stem and leaves from artichokes and cut out bottom; scrape away choke. Quarter artichoke bottoms and boil in salted water 3 to 4 minutes, then drain and cool. Blanch tomatoes briefly in boiling water. Drain, seed, and dice. Peel and chop onion. Heat oil in flameproof baking dish large enough to hold fish; sauté onion until tender. Place fish on top and cook on top of stove 2 minutes. Remove from heat, turn fish, and add artichoke pieces and tomato. Season with salt and pepper and pour in wine. Bake on middle rack of preheated 400°F (200°C) oven for 10 minutes. Pour cream over, sprinkle with herbs, and bake until fish is cooked through, about 10 more minutes.

Stuffed Sardines

Fresh sardines, which can sometimes be found at large fish markets, are well worth hunting for. This dish is popular in southern France and in Spain; serve it with crusty French bread.

4 servings
2¹/₂ pounds (1200 g) fresh sardines (about 20)
Salt
1 small onion
1 clove garlic
8 ounces (250 g) trimmed fresh spinach
2 tablespoons vegetable oil
3 tablespoons white wine
¹/₂ teaspoon salt
Freshly ground pepper
¹/₂ cup (60 g) pine nuts
3 tablespoons (50 g) butter
³/₄ cup (60 g) breadcrumbs

Using a small pair of shears, cut open sardines and remove entrails and heads. Grasp backbone with thumb and index finger at cut end; hold fish firmly with the other hand and slowly pull out backbone. Spread fish out on work surface skin side down. Peel and dice onion. Peel and crush garlic. Wash spinach leaves and drain well.

Heat oil in large saucepan. Add onion and garlic and sauté until tender. Add spinach, wine, salt, and pepper, then cover and cook 4 to 5 minutes. Coarsely chop pine nuts and stir into spinach mixture.

Salt sardines very lightly and spread with spinach. Starting at cut ends, roll up fish so that tail lies on top. Melt half of butter in large flameproof baking dish. Arrange sardine rolls in dish; sprinkle with breadcrumbs and dot with remaining butter. Bake on middle rack of preheated 400°F (200°C) oven for 12 to 15 minutes.

Sarde a Beccafico

Not illustrated

For this Sicilian specialty the sardines are prepared as in the preceding recipe; only the stuffing is different.

4 servings
2¹/₄ pounds (1 kg) fresh sardines
Salt
1 clove garlic
3 tablespoons olive oil
1 tablespoon diced onion
2 tablespoons chopped fresh parsley
1¹/₂ cups (150 g) breadcrumbs
Salt and freshly ground pepper
¹/₂ cup (50 g) pine nuts
³/₄ cup (100 g) freshly grated pecorino Romano cheese

Prepare sardines as in preceding recipe; salt very lightly. Peel and crush garlic.

Heat olive oil in skillet. Add onion and garlic and sauté until tender. Remove tails from 2 cleaned sardines, add fish to skillet, and mash with fork. Add parsley, breadcrumbs, salt, and pepper and cook, stirring, until crumbs are lightly colored, 3 to 4 minutes. Remove from heat. Coarsely chop pine nuts and stir into breadcrumb mixture with grated cheese. Divide stuffing among sardines and roll up. Spread some olive oil in large baking dish and arrange sardine rolls in dish. Bake on middle rack of preheated 400°F (200°C) oven for 12 to 15 minutes.

Perch with Leeks and Shrimp

Best made with single-portion-size fish or with those weighing 1¹/₄ to 1¹/₂ pounds (600 to 700 g), which will serve two. Accompany this with crusty bread.

2 servings
1 cleaned whole perch, mullet, or croaker (1 to 1¹/₄ pounds/ 600 to 700 g)
Salt and freshly ground pepper
2 tablespoons chopped fresh herbs (parsley, lovage or celery leaves, oregano, and a little rosemary)
¹/₂ chili pepper
Juice of ¹/₂ lemon or lime
2 medium leeks
3 tablespoons (40 g) butter
¹/₂ small onion
5 ounces (150 g) cooked, peeled shrimp
¹/₂ cup (125 mL) dry white wine

Scale the cleaned fish (see page 20) and trim away fins. Cut parallel slashes ¹/₂ inch (1 cm) deep in each side of fish (see photograph) to promote even cooking. Season inside and out with salt, pepper, and herbs. Seed and mince chili pepper and scatter into fish. Sprinkle with lemon or lime juice, wrap in foil, and let fish stand 1 hour to absorb flavors.

Trim and carefully wash leeks. If leeks are very slender, cut into 2-inch (5-cm) pieces; cut thicker leeks into slices. Peel and chop onion. Melt butter in ovenproof saucepan or skillet large enough to hold fish. Add onion and sauté until light golden. Add leek and cook, stirring frequently, 5 to 6 minutes. Add fish and shrimp to pan and pour wine over. Bake on middle rack of preheated 400°F (200°C) oven for 20 to 25 minutes, basting with pan juices from time to time. Season with salt and pepper.

Baked Sea Bass

Photo on the cover

2 servings
1 whole sea bass (1¹/₄ pounds/ 600 g)
Salt and freshly ground pepper
1 teaspoon fresh lime juice
1 small onion
¹/₂ clove garlic
3 tablespoons vegetable oil
1 zucchini
2 small tomatoes
1 tablespoon chopped fresh herbs (parsley, basil, and chives)
2 tablespoons dry white wine
4 ounces (120 g) cooked, peeled shrimp

Clean fish, scale (see page 20), and trim away fins. Season fish inside and out with salt and pepper; sprinkle with lime juice. Peel and chop onion; peel and crush garlic.

Heat oil in flameproof baking dish large enough to hold fish.

Add onion and garlic and sauté until tender. Scrub zucchini under cold running water, trim ends, and slice thinly. Add to onion and cook 2 to 3 minutes. Meanwhile, blanch tomatoes in boiling water; peel, seed, and cut into wedges. Add to baking dish. Cut slashes in each side of fish to promote even cooking. Lay fish atop vegetables, sprinkle with wine, and add shrimp. Bake on middle rack of preheated 400°F (200°C) oven for 20 to 25 minutes.

Herbed Trout Terrine

Trout, pike, perch, halibut, turbot, sea bass, and monkfish are all particularly good in fish terrines.

6 to 8 servings

12 ounces (400 g) trout fillets (from cleaned whole trout weighing about 1 1/2 pounds/ 700 g)

2 slices firm white bread, crusts trimmed

2 egg whites

1 cup + 2 tablespoons (275 mL) whipping or heavy cream

1/2 teaspoon salt

Freshly ground pepper

Pinch each of ground ginger and allspice

Grated lemon peel

1 teaspoon fresh lemon juice

2 tablespoons chopped fresh herbs (parsley, chervil, lemon balm, tarragon, sweet woodruff, and dill)

7 ounces (200 g) cooked, peeled shrimp

For the aspic

1 envelope unflavored gelatin

1/4 cup (60 mL) water

1/2 cup (60 mL) dry white wine

1 1/2 tablespoons medium-dry Sherry

A few drops of Cognac

Salt and freshly ground pepper

Fresh herbs as desired for decoration (parsley, dill, sweet woodruff, tarragon, tiny slices of beet green)

Wash cleaned fish well under running water and pat dry with paper towels. Cut away head, tail, and fins. Make a slit along backbone of fish with sharp knife and carefully lift fillets away from bones. Use tweezers to remove any bones remaining in fillets. Lay fillets on work surface skin side down and insert knife between skin and flesh, then remove fillets with one sharp tug.

Cut fillets into pieces and place in bowl. Dice bread and add to fish. Beat 1 egg white with 2 tablespoons cream, salt, pepper, ginger, allspice, a bit of grated lemon peel, and the lemon juice. Pour over fish and bread and refrigerate at least 2 hours.

Puree in processor or blender in small batches to prevent mixture from warming up. Refrigerate until well chilled, then strain through fine sieve. Return to refrigerator.

Meanwhile, combine remaining egg white and 1 cup (240 mL) cream and beat to stiff peaks. Stir into fish mixture in small portions. Set bowl of fish puree into larger bowl of ice. Divide mixture in half; stir herbs into one half. Butter 1-quart

(1-L) terrine. Spread herbed fish paste into terrine in two layers, dotting first layer with shrimp. Repeat with plain mixture, again arranging shrimp on first layer. Smooth top and cover terrine. Pour water into pot large enough to hold terrine; water should reach 3/4 inch (2 cm) below terrine rim. Set terrine aside.

Preheat oven to 300°F (150°C). Place pot of water in oven and heat to 175°F (80°C) (if you do not have a thermometer, heat water for 20 to 30 minutes). Place terrine in heated water and bake 40 minutes. Let cool slowly in water bath, then lift terrine out and refrigerate until well chilled.

To prepare aspic, soften gelatin in water. Heat wine to just below boiling point. Season with Sherry, Cognac, salt, and pepper. Add softened gelatin and stir until dissolved. Decorate top of terrine with herbs and carefully pour aspic over. If necessary, refrigerate briefly to firm.

FISH AND VEGETABLES

Perch Fillets with Zucchini

Freshwater fish and garden-fresh vegetables make a wonderful combination, especially during the summer and fall months when both are in season. Take care to team mild-flavored fish such as perch, pike, or trout with comparably mild vegetables—tender carrots, cucumbers, zucchini, or fresh asparagus.

2 servings
1 whole perch (about 1 1/4 pounds/600 g)
1 medium carrot
1 large leek
1/2 medium celery root
1 small parsley root
1 1/2 cups (350 mL) water
2 medium zucchini
3 tablespoons (50 g) butter
1/2 teaspoon salt
Freshly ground pepper
1 teaspoon fresh thyme leaves
1/4 cup (60 mL) dry white wine
For the tomato accompaniment
2 plum tomatoes
1 teaspoon butter
Salt and freshly ground pepper

Clean fish, rinse briefly under running water, fillet, and skin (see pages 20 and 23). Thoroughly wash head, bones, and skin. Trim and wash carrot, leek, celery root, and parsley root. Combine fish trimmings, vegetables, and water in large saucepan and prepare fish stock as described on page 9. Strain stock through fine sieve, return to saucepan, and simmer until reduced to about 1/2 cup (125 mL).

Wash and trim zucchini; cut into 3/4-inch (2-cm) slices. Melt half of butter in skillet large enough to hold fish and vegetables. Add zucchini and cook 2 to 3 minutes. Season with salt, pepper, and thyme. Pour in fish stock and wine. Lay fish fillets on top, cover, and simmer gently 2 to 3 minutes. Uncover and cook another 2 to 3 minutes. Dot with remaining butter and distribute by shaking pan carefully. Simmer gently for 2 to 3 minutes longer.

Meanwhile, blanch tomatoes in boiling water; peel and seed. Dice flesh and stew briefly in butter, shaking pan constantly. Season with salt and pepper. Serve stewed tomatoes with fish.

Dilled Halibut and Cucumbers

Not illustrated

4 servings
4 halibut fillets (about 7 ounces/ 200 g each)
Fresh lemon juice
Salt
1 small onion
1 medium carrot
2 tablespoons (30 g) butter
Freshly ground pepper
1 generous pound (500 g) cucumbers
1/2 cup (125 mL) dry white wine
2 tablespoons chopped fresh dill

Pat fish fillets dry with paper towels. Sprinkle with lemon juice and season with salt. Peel and mince onion; trim and finely dice carrot.

Melt butter in large skillet with tight-fitting lid. Add onion and sauté until tender. Add carrot and cook 2 to 3 minutes. Season with 1/2 teaspoon salt and pepper to taste. Peel cucumbers and halve lengthwise. Remove seeds. Cut cucumbers into sticks about 1/3 inch (1 cm) thick and 1 1/4 inches (3 cm) long. Add to skillet, pour wine over, and cook over gentle heat for 5 to 6 minutes. Sprinkle with dill, lay fish fillets on top, cover, and cook over medium heat 8 to 10 minutes.

Turbot with Baby Vegetables

Turbot is one of the very highest-quality fish, well worth using in painstaking preparations such as this one. Because of its mild flavor, turbot is best cooked in a well-seasoned stock—not in plain water. The same stock can then be used to make a sauce for the finished dish, a technique that is useful with many varieties of fish. Accompany this with new potatoes and serve the same wine that was used for the cooking.

If you purchase a whole turbot and fillet it yourself, use the trimmings to make a stock as described on page 9. If you have frozen fish stock on hand the preparation will be that much simpler.

4 servings
3 small leeks
2 small zucchini
3 ounces (100 g) baby carrots
1 tablespoon (20 g) butter
3/4 cup (100 g) shelled fresh peas
1/4 cup (60 mL) meat stock or water
1/2 teaspoon salt
Freshly ground pepper

For the fish
2 tablespoons (30 g) butter
1 1/4 pounds (600 g) turbot fillets (4 pieces, about 5 ounces/ 150 g each)
1/2 cup (125 mL) dry white wine
1 1/2 cups (350 mL) fish stock (see recipe, page 9)
1 teaspoon fresh lemon juice
1/2 teaspoon salt
1 sprig tarragon
For the sauce
1 egg yolk
1/2 cup (125 mL) whipping or heavy cream
Fresh chervil or tarragon leaves

Trim leeks and wash thoroughly; cut into small pieces. Scrub zucchini and carrots under running water and cut into thin julienne. Melt butter in saucepan, add prepared vegetables and peas, and stir over high heat 1 minute. Pour in stock or water, season with salt and pepper, and cook until liquid is almost completely evaporated and vegetables are crisp-tender, about 4 to 5 minutes.

Grease a large skillet or saucepan with the butter. Lay fish fillets in pan and pour wine, fish stock, and lemon juice over. Season with salt and tarragon sprig. Cover and place over medium heat until liquid begins to boil, then reduce heat and simmer 1 minute. Turn off heat and let fish rest in liquid, covered, for 10 minutes.

Pour off 1 cup (240 mL) cooking liquid and boil slowly until reduced by about 2/3. Divide fillets and vegetables among 4 plates. Combine egg yolk and cream and beat to soft peaks with whisk or portable mixer. Whisk into reduced fish stock and immediately spoon over fish. Sprinkle with chervil or tarragon leaves and serve.

Scallops au Gratin

The quantities used in this recipe are sufficient for four first-course or light supper servings. For a more substantial main course, double the amounts and serve two filled shells per person. If the scallops will be a first course, accompany with crusty bread; if a main dish, serve with saffron rice and the same wine used in the sauce (a German or Alsatian Riesling would be ideal). The scallop mixture can also be gratinéed on flameproof plates if shells are not available.

4 servings
4 sea scallops, preferably with roe
1 cup (240 mL) milk
4 sole fillets
Salt and freshly ground pepper
7 ounces (200 g) fresh spinach
Freshly grated nutmeg
4 scallop shells
3 tablespoons (40 g) butter, softened
1 tablespoon coarsely chopped fresh chervil

For the sauce
1 tablespoon vegetable oil
1 tablespoon minced shallot
$1/2$ cup (125 mL) fish stock (see recipe, page 9)
$1/2$ cup (125 mL) dry white wine
$1 1/2$ tablespoons dry vermouth
3 tablespoons (50 g) butter, chilled
1 egg yolk
3 tablespoons (50 g) crème fraîche

Rinse scallops in cold water and pat dry. Place in bowl, cover with milk, cover, and refrigerate at least 12 hours.

Spread out sole fillets on work surface, season very lightly with salt and pepper, and roll up. Secure rolls with toothpicks.

Wash and pick over spinach. Bring a large quantity of salted water to boil, add spinach, and cook just until wilted. Drain well and season with nutmeg and pepper.

Scrub scallop shells and dry thoroughly. Grease generously with the softened butter. Divide spinach among shells. Top each with 1 scallop, 1 portion of roe, and a sole roulade. Sprinkle with chervil.

For the sauce, heat oil in small saucepan. Add shallot and sauté until tender. Pour in fish stock, wine, and vermouth and cook over medium heat, stirring frequently, until reduced to about $1/3$ cup (75 mL). Whisk in chilled butter a few pieces at a time. Whisk egg yolk with crème fraîche and blend into sauce.

Place scallop shells under preheated broiler for 4 to 5 minutes, then cover with sauce and cook until flecked with golden brown, another 6 to 8 minutes. Serve immediately.

FISH FROM THE GRILL

Grilled Sardines

Grilling is an excellent cooking method for fish, provided you observe several important guidelines. Many kinds are best grilled whole so that the tender flesh is protected by the skin. The most suitable types for grilling are those with very firm flesh, such as swordfish, tuna, and salmon; these can also be cut into steaks before grilling, or even—a typical treatment for tuna—cubed and threaded on skewers (see recipe on page 74).

Oily fish such as herring, mackerel, and eel do not need any special treatment to keep from drying out over a hot fire. This is not the case with lean fish, which must be basted frequently with oil or an oil-based marinade during grilling. An aluminum foil wrapping also protects fish from high grill temperatures—a modern version of the old-fashioned technique of wrapping fish in grape leaves. (Usually, a leaf wrap is only suitable for smaller fish, but in the tropics an enormous banana leaf is sometimes used for larger ones.) Fish grilled in leaves remains very juicy, in part because of the moisture contained in the leaves themselves.

4 servings
16 sardines (2 to 3 ounces/70 to 80 g each)
6 tablespoons olive or vegetable oil
Salt and freshly ground pepper

Make a slit along belly of each sardine with small scissors; remove entrails and wash fish briefly. Pat dry with paper towels and make several parallel slashes on both sides. Season generously with salt and pepper and brush both sides with oil. Place sardines over heated coals and grill 2 to 3 minutes on each side. Distance from the heat source should depend on the size of the fish; grill small sardines 2 inches (5 cm) above the coals and larger sardines 4 to 6 inches (10 to 15 cm) or more above the coals, so that the outside does not burn before the flesh is cooked through.

Variation

Sardines can be wrapped in grape leaves and cooked according to the same recipe; the result will be particularly tender. When possible, use fresh grape leaves picked right off the vine. If these are not available, bottled leaves can be substituted; if very salty, rinse them first. Oil the sardines as in the master recipe, wrap in the leaves, and grill on both sides. Cooking time may be very slightly increased.

Eel in Grape Leaves

Steeping the eel in a spicy marinade before wrapping it in grape leaves gives the flesh a delicious piquancy. Aluminum foil can be substituted for the leaves if you wish.

4 servings
2 cleaned eels (1 pound/450 g each)
Grape leaves (fresh or bottled) or foil for wrapping
For the marinade
1/2 cup (125 mL) vegetable oil
Juice of l lemon
1 small onion
2 cloves garlic
2 fresh chili peppers
1 large carrot
2 stalks celery
1 tablespoon chopped capers
1 tablespoon chopped fresh parsley
1 teaspoon salt
Freshly ground pepper

If you cannot purchase dressed eel, buy the eel whole and clean it as described on page 80. Cut eel into pieces about 2 inches (5 to 6 cm) long.

For the marinade, whisk oil and lemon juice in large non-aluminum bowl. Peel and finely chop onion and garlic. Seed and finely chop chilies. Trim and finely dice carrot and celery. Add prepared vegetables to oil mixture with capers, parsley, salt, and pepper and mix well. Add eel pieces and stir to coat. Let marinate at least 2 hours, preferably longer.

Spread out leaves on work surface; if using bottled grape leaves, drain well (rinse first if very salty). Wrap marinated eel and vegetables in leaves, using 1 to 2 per piece of eel depending on size of leaves. To keep packets from opening on grill, tie each one closed with cotton thread or secure with a toothpick. Grill packets over hot coals for 8 to 10 minutes on each side.

Grilled Mackerel

Small mackerel are also excellent prepared according to the method described in the previous recipe. Not illustrated.

4 servings
4 cleaned whole small mackerel (10 ounces/300 g each)
Marinade from previous recipe
4 thyme sprigs
Grape leaves for wrapping

Wash mackerel briefly under running water and pat thoroughly dry with paper towels. Cut 4 or 5 parallel slashes in each side of fish to help marinade penetrate. Place fish in large nonaluminum bowl, cover with marinade, and let stand at least 2 hours. Remove mackerel from marinade and wrap with vegetables (as for eel) in overlapping vine leaves. Grill over hot coals for 8 to 9 minutes on each side.

Tuna with Lemon Sauce

Tuna is perfect for grilling because its firm flesh stays juicy and does not fall apart. Steaks cut from fish between 16 and 32 inches (40 to 80 cm) long are easiest to work with, but a good market will also be able to cut usable steaks from larger fish. Grilled tomatoes, seasoned simply with salt and pepper, make an excellent side dish.

4 servings
4 tuna steaks (7 ounces/200 g each)
For the marinade
2 tablespoons finely chopped onion
1 teaspoon coarsely cracked black pepper
2 bay leaves
1 sprig rosemary
1 sprig thyme
1/2 cup (125 mL) olive oil
For the sauce
1/2 cup (125 mL) fish stock (see recipe, page 9)
3 tablespoons dry white wine
1 1/2 tablespoons fresh lemon juice
Peel of 1 lemon, cut into very fine julienne
1/4 cup (50 g) crème fraîche

Rinse tuna steaks under running water, pat dry, and place in large bowl.

Peel and crush garlic. Sprinkle fish with onion, garlic, and pepper. Break bay leaves in half and add to bowl with rosemary and thyme sprigs. Pour in olive oil, turn steaks to coat evenly, cover, and marinate at least 2 to 3 hours. Remove steaks from marinade (don't worry about any clinging bits of onion or herbs) and set on a rack to drain; enough oil will remain on fish to protect it during grilling. Cook fish over hot coals for 6 to 7 minutes on each side.

For the sauce, combine fish stock, wine, and lemon juice in nonaluminum saucepan and boil gently until reduced by half. Stir in lemon peel and crème fraîche. Let stand in a warm place for a few minutes for flavors to blend, then serve with fish.

Tuna Kebabs

Not illustrated

Serve with a tossed green salad.

4 servings
1 1/4 pounds (600 g) fresh tuna steaks
3 ounces (100 g) small boiling onions
1 red bell pepper
3 ounces (100 g) mushrooms
For the marinade
1 fresh chili pepper
1 clove garlic
1/2 cup (125 mL) vegetable oil
2 teaspoons fresh lemon juice
1/2 teaspoon salt
1 tablespoon chopped mixed fresh herbs (choose according to taste)

Cut fish into cubes. Trim and peel onions. Seed bell pepper and cut into pieces. Trim and wash mushrooms.

Alternate tuna with onions, bell pepper pieces, and mushrooms on 4 skewers. Lay in large bowl or dish. Seed and finely chop chili pepper. Peel and crush garlic. Mix oil with lemon juice, salt, chili, garlic, and herbs. Pour over kebabs and let marinate 2 to 3 hours.

Remove kebabs from marinade and drain. Grill 4 to 6 minutes on each side.

ROASTED, BRAISED, AND STEWED

Baked Haddock

The roasting bag is perfect for preparing fish, because it cooks in its own juices without added liquid or fat. Using this technique, a fish tastes fresh and flavorful without so much as a single other ingredient—in the case of saltwater types, even salt is unnecessary because the flesh itself contains enough. Of course, the fish can also be seasoned with herbs or vegetables; the possible combinations are virtually limitless. In this case, accompany the fish with the vegetables from the roasting bag, and with boiled potatoes or French bread if you wish.

4 servings
1 haddock, head removed (about 1³/4 pounds/800 g)
1 zucchini
1 medium carrot
2 large green onions
1 bouquet garni (1 sprig each parsley, thyme, and lovage or celery leaves)
3 tablespoons dry white wine
¹/2 teaspoon salt

Wash fish briefly under running water and pat dry with paper towels. Trim away fins with kitchen shears. Place fish in roasting bag. Scrub zucchini under running water and slice thinly. Trim, peel, and thinly slice carrot. Trim green onions and cut into pieces. Arrange vegetables around fish. Add bouquet garni and wine and sprinkle salt over all ingredients. Close bag and set into roasting pan. Place in preheated 425°F (220°C) oven until fish is cooked through, about 25 to 30 minutes.

Cut the roasting bag open at the table; a sensational aroma will escape.

Roasting bags are available in several sizes; choose one that fits the ingredients comfortably.

Tip: Here are some tips for cooking in a roasting bag. After filling the bag and closing off the end, pierce the top of the bag once with a fork or several times with a needle. Place in a cold roasting pan, then slide into the preheated oven.

Unlike aluminum foil or standard cooking vessels, a roasting bag permits heat to penetrate the food unhindered. The holes pierced in the top keep the pressure inside from becoming excessive, while the steam that forms moderates the temperature in the bag: It will be no more than 300°F (150°C) or so even when the oven is set at 425°F (220°C).

This cooking method is great for preserving nutrients and flavor, for no juices are lost and it is not necessary to add a lot of liquid.

Halibut with Saffron Risotto

Photo, bottom

4 servings
1 lemon
1 small onion
1 medium carrot
10 ounces (300 g) mussels
1 bay leaf
2 tablespoons vegetable oil
Salt and freshly ground pepper
4 halibut fillets (5 to 7 ounces/150 to 200 g each)
1/2 cup (125 mL) dry white wine
1 cup (240 mL) fish stock (see recipe, page 9)
For the risotto
2 tablespoons (30 g) butter
1 tablespoon finely chopped onion
Pinch of garlic powder
Salt and freshly ground pepper
3/4 cup (150 g) short-grain rice (preferably Arborio)
1/2 cup (125 mL) dry white wine
2 cups (450 mL) fish stock
A few saffron threads or a pinch of powdered saffron

Peel lemon and onion, trim carrot, and very thinly slice all three. Carefully clean and debeard mussels, discarding any that are open.

Heat oil in large skillet with tight-fitting lid. Add onion, car-rot, and lemon slices, crushed bay leaf, salt, and pepper. Lay fish fillets on top and pour wine and fish stock over. Arrange mussels atop fish. Cover and bring liquid to boil, then imme-diately reduce heat to low and cook 3 minutes. Uncover skillet; mussels should be opened. Remove mussels and continue cooking fish over low heat for 8 to 10 minutes.

For the risotto, melt butter in saucepan, add onion and sauté until tender. Add garlic powder, salt, pepper, and rice and stir several minutes over high heat. Pour in wine and cook 1 to 2 minutes. Add fish stock and saf-fron and simmer gently over moderate heat until rice is ten-der but still firm to bite, about 20 minutes. Remove fish and mus-sels from skillet and keep warm. Strain cooking liquid over risotto and cook 1 to 2 minutes longer. Divide rice among 4 plates, arrange fish and mussels alongside rice, and serve imme-diately.

Halibut in Mushroom Risotto

Photo, top

4 servings
2 tablespoons (30 g) butter
2 tablespoons finely chopped onion
1 clove garlic
3/4 cup (150 g) short-grain rice (preferably Arborio)
1/2 cup (125 mL) dry white wine
2 cups (450 mL) chicken stock
1/2 teaspoon salt
Freshly ground pepper
7 ounces (200 g) mushrooms
1 generous pound (500 g) halibut fillets
2 tablespoons (30 g) butter
1/3 cup (40 g) freshly grated Parmesan cheese

Melt butter in large saucepan, add onion and sauté until ten-der. Peel garlic and add to skillet with rice; stir for several minutes over high heat. Pour in wine and cook several more minutes, stir-ring. Add chicken stock, season with salt and pepper, and cook for 10 minutes.

Trim, clean, and thinly slice mushrooms. Add to rice and cook over medium heat for 15 minutes.

Place fish on top of risotto and simmer for several minutes. Break fish into smaller pieces and cook over very low heat for a few more minutes, just until fish is opaque. Dot with butter and top witn cheese. Stir through gently and serve.

Fresh Eel Brabant Style

This preparation method, popular in Belgium and Holland, is especially well suited to the rich, flavorful meat of eel. If possible, choose eels weighing about 1¹/₂ pounds (700 g), as smaller ones have too much waste in proportion to meat and larger eels tend to be fatty.

If the eel is not already skinned when you buy it, the procedure is not all that difficult—though it does take some practice. Lay the gutted eel on its back on the work surface. Using a sharp knife, cut through the meat and backbone underneath the small fins at the head, without cutting all the way through the skin. With a paring knife, separate the skin from the meat for a little over an inch (3 cm), or enough to get a good hold on the skin. Sprinkle your hands with salt for better grip. Firmly grasp the skinned portion of the eel with your right hand; with the left, hold the head with attached skin and pull back toward the tail with one sharp tug to strip off the skin. Though this maneuver may at first seem risky, don't let it alarm you; the skin is no stronger than the flesh, and the eel will not tear apart.

4 servings
2¹/₄ pounds (1 kg) cleaned, skinned eel (about 3 pounds/ 1400 g with head and skin)
¹/₄ cup (60 g) butter
¹/₂ teaspoon salt
1 cup (50 g) sorrel
1 tablespoon chopped fresh chervil
1 tablespoon chopped fresh tarragon
1 tablespoon chopped fresh dill
1 tablespoon fresh lemon juice
¹/₂ cup (125 mL) fish stock (see recipe, page 9) or water
¹/₂ cup (125 mL) white wine
1 bay leaf
1 egg yolk

Hold open the slit through which eel was gutted and wash inside carefully under running water. Cut eel into 2-inch (5-cm) pieces.

Melt butter in large saucepan. Season eel with salt, add to saucepan, and sauté 3 to 4 minutes. Coarsely chop sorrel and add to eel with chervil, tarragon, and dill. Sprinkle with lemon juice; pour in fish stock and wine. Add bay leaf and cook over low heat 10 to 15 minutes, depending on thickness of eel. Remove 2 tablespoons cooking liquid and whisk with egg yolk. Stir back into saucepan and cook over low heat, stirring, for 1 to 2 more minutes; do not boil or sauce will curdle.

Flounder in Red Wine

According to the old rules, the question of whether to pair fish with red or white wine never arose; traditionally, only white was used. But it had to be of the right type, namely light and dry—because a syrupy sweet white wine is in fact less compatible with fish than a light, dry red. On the other hand, as long as a red wine is not overly tannic it is well suited to fish cookery and as an accompanying beverage. This recipe is a good example: Here a light, fruity Beaujolais makes a perfect partner for the fish. Parsleyed potatoes make a good side dish.

4 servings
4 cleaned flounder (10 ounces/300 g each)
1 medium onion
1 large carrot
2 stalks celery
2 tablespoons (30 g) butter
2 cups (450 mL) Beaujolais
1 bouquet garni (parsley, tarragon, and lemon balm)
4 lemon or lime wedges

For the fish stock
1 package soup greens
1/2 teaspoon salt
3 cups (700 mL) water

For the sauce
1 small shallot
1 tablespoon (20 g) butter
Salt and freshly ground pepper
1/2 cup (125 mL) crème fraîche

Remove fins and heads from cleaned flounder and wash well to use for fish stock. Trim soup greens. Combine fish trimmings, soup greens, salt, and water in large saucepan and prepare fish stock as described on page 9.

Peel and slice onion; trim and finely dice carrot and celery. Butter a flameproof baking dish large enough to hold fish in overlapping layers. Spread vegetables evenly in bottom. Lay fish on top of vegetables and pour in wine and strained fish stock. Add bouquet garni, cover, and bring to simmer on top of stove. Meanwhile, preheat oven to 400°F (200°C). Uncover dish and bake fish 10 to 12 minutes. Remove flounder and transfer to serving platter; keep warm. Simmer cooking liquid on top of stove until reduced by half.

For the sauce, peel and mince shallot. Melt butter, add shallot, and sauté until tender. Season with salt and pepper. Strain reduced fish stock into shallot through fine sieve and boil gently until reduced to a maximum of 1 cup (240 mL). Whisk in crème fraîche and heat through, stirring. Serve sauce with fish and garnish with lemon or lime wedge.

SMOKED FISH SPECIALTIES

Smoked Fish Skillet

The following two recipes show that smoked fish doesn't always have to be eaten cold: When partnered witn the right ingredients, it is also delicious warm. Smoked fish goes especially well with eggs, as this recipe demonstrates.

4 servings
1 medium onion
1 small zucchini
1 red bell pepper
2 tablespoons (30 g) butter
1/2 teaspoon salt
Freshly ground pepper
8 ounces (250 g) smoked halibut or other smoked fish
7 ounces (200 g) Schillerlocken (smoked fillet of sea eel)* or other smoked fish
For the eggs
4 eggs
Salt and freshly ground pepper
1 tablespoon snipped fresh chives
1 tablespoon chopped fresh parsley

*Available at German delicatessens and butcher shops.

Peel and mince onion. Scrub and trim zucchini; slice thinly. Seed and wash bell pepper and cut into thin strips. Peel and dice potatoes. Melt butter in skillet. Add onion and sauté briefly. Add zucchini, pepper strips, and potato; season with salt and pepper, and cook over medium heat 3 to 4 minutes.

Meanwhile, shred halibut by hand into small pieces. Cut *Schillerlocken* into slices 1/2 inch (1 cm) thick. Add to skillet and heat for several minutes, stirring frequently.

Whisk eggs and season with salt and pepper. Blend in chives and parsley. Pour over mixture in skillet and cook over very low heat until eggs are set. Serve immediately.

Smoked Trout with Artichokes and Gorgonzola

Not illustrated

4 servings
2 smoked trout (12 ounces/ 350 g each)
1 small onion
2 tablespoons (30 g) butter
7 ounces (200 g) canned or bottled artichoke hearts
Salt and freshly ground pepper
2 eggs
3 ounces (80 g) Gorgonzola cheese
2 tablespoons snipped fresh chives

Fillet the trout. Peel and finely dice onion. Melt butter in skillet and sauté onion until tender. Drain artichoke hearts well; quarter and add to skillet. Season with salt and pepper and cook, stirring, 3 to 4 minutes.

Whisk eggs. Finely dice cheese and mix into eggs with chives. Lay trout fillets in skillet, pour egg mixture over, and cook over very low heat until eggs are set. Adjust seasoning with salt and pepper and serve.

DEEP-FRIED FISH

Batter-fried Cod

Photo, bottom

Fish and shellfish remain juicy and flavorful when deep-fried in a batter coating. Use firm-fleshed fish, or shellfish such as shrimp, mussels or squid.

4 servings
8 cod steaks (about 3 ounces/100 g each)
Juice of 1/2 lemon
Salt and freshly ground pepper
1 1/4 cups (150 g) flour
1/4 teaspoon salt
Freshly ground pepper
1 egg
2 tablespoons vegetable oil
1 cup (240 mL) light beer or water (approximately)
Vegetable oil for deep-frying
For the sauce
7 tablespoons (100 g) crème fraîche
Pinch of cayenne pepper
1 tablespoon fresh lemon juice
2 tablespoons chopped fresh herbs (lemon balm, lovage or celery leaves, parsley, tarragon, and thyme)
Salt (optional)
1/4 cup (60 mL) whipping or heavy cream, whipped

The fish steaks should not be too thick or they will not cook evenly. Sprinkle fish lightly with lemon juice; season with salt and pepper.

Sift flour into wide bowl. Mix in salt, pepper, egg, oil, and enough beer or water to make a smooth, thick but flowing batter. Stir until all lumps have disappeared. (The result will vary according to the amount of liquid added; a thick batter will form a substantial coating on the fish, while a thin one will be light and crisp after frying.) Let batter rest 1 hour.

For the sauce, mix crème fraîche with cayenne, lemon juice, and herbs. Season with salt if necessary. Fold in whipped cream.

Heat oil for deep frying to 350°F (180°C). Spear each fish piece on fork and dip into batter, being sure fish is thoroughly coated. Deep-fry in batches for 3 to 4 minutes on each side. Remove with slotted spoon and drain well on paper towels. Serve with sauce.

Fried Calamari

Photo, top

Serve with a tossed green salad.

4 servings
1 1/2 pounds (750 g) fresh small squid (calamari)
1 1/4 cups (150 g) flour
1 egg yolk
1/4 teaspoon salt
Freshly ground pepper
2 tablespoons vegetable oil
1 cup (240 mL) light beer
2 egg whites
Vegetable oil
Parsley sprigs and lemon wedges

Rinse squid well under running water. Cut away tentacles and reserve in one piece. Discard beak, clear "quill" and ink sac. Peel away skin and cut body of squid into 1/2-inch (1-cm) rings. Drain all pieces well on paper towels. Prepare batter as in previous recipe and let stand for 1 hour, then beat 1 egg white until stiff peaks form and fold into batter.

Heat oil for deep-frying to 350°F (180°C). Using a fork, dip squid pieces into batter, place in hot oil, and fry until crisp and golden, 4 to 5 minutes, turning frequently. Remove and drain on paper towels. Garnish with parsley and lemon wedges and serve.

ONE-DISH MEALS

Sailors' Stew

For fish and shellfish stews choose the seafoods (at least three kinds) that are most readily available; it is not essential to use the particular types listed here.

4 servings
1 large onion
1 small celery root
1 large carrot
3 tablespoons vegetable oil
3 cups (700 mL) water or fish stock (see recipe, page 9)
1 tablespoon sweet paprika
1/2 teaspoon salt
Freshly ground pepper
1 generous pound (500 g) cod fillets
1 generous pound (500 g) cleaned mackerel
1 generous pound (500 g) mussels
1 tablespoon chopped fresh parsley
2/3 cup (150 g) crème fraîche or sour cream

Peel and finely chop onion. Trim and dice celery root and carrot. Peel and crush garlic. Heat oil in large saucepan. Add vegetables and sauté over medium-high heat until tender. Pour in water or fish stock, season with paprika, salt, and pepper, and simmer 10 to 12 minutes.

Rinse cod fillets and cut into cubes. Rinse mackerel well under running water. Cut away head, tail, and fins and cut fish into large pieces. Scrub and debeard mussels (discard any open ones) and steam briefly until they open; discard any mussels that do not open. Add cod and mackerel to vegetable mixture and simmer 5 minutes. Add mussels and cook over very low heat for 5 more minutes; liquid should barely bubble. Remove from heat and sprinkle with parsley. Carefully stir in crème fraîche or sour cream and serve.

Seafood One-Pot

Photo on title page

4 servings
1 medium onion
1 large carrot
1 large leek
1/2 large celery root
3 tablespoons vegetable oil
2 cups (450 mL) fish stock (see recipe, page 9)
1/2 cup (125 mL) dry white wine
10 ounces (300 g) squid
10 ounces lingcod or other firm fish fillets
4 shelled prawns or crayfish
8 ounces (250 g) mussels
4 to 6 hard-shelled clams, such as littlenecks
1 tablespoon chopped fresh parsley
1 tablespoon chopped fresh dill
1/2 teaspoon salt
Freshly ground pepper

Peel and finely dice onion. Trim and finely chop carrot, leek, and celery root. Heat oil in large saucepan. Add vegetables and sauté over medium-high heat 3 to 4 minutes. Pour in fish stock and wine and bring to simmer. Carefully clean squid (see page 86); cut tentacles and bodies into pieces. Add to stock mixture and simmer 2 to 3 minutes. Briefly rinse fish, cut into cubes, and add to saucepan with prawns; poach over very low heat 4 to 5 minutes. Scrub and debeard mussels, discarding any opened ones; scrub clams. Steam mussels and clams until shells open, as in preceding recipe, and add to saucepan. Sprinkle with parsley and dill, season with salt and pepper and poach gently another 5 to 6 minutes. Serve immediately.

88

MARINATED FISH

Marinated Sardines

It is a time-honored European tradition to pickle cooked small fish such as sardines and herring. Many fresh- and saltwater species, as well as shellfish, lend themselves to this treatment. Serve the fish for a light summer supper or as a first course.

4 servings
1¹/₂ pounds (750 g) fresh sardines
Flour
¹/₂ cup (125 mL) olive oil
Salt and freshly ground pepper
¹/₂ large onion
1 clove garlic
1 to 2 small red chili peppers
¹/₂ cup (125 mL) water
¹/₂ cup (125 mL) dry white wine
2 teaspoons balsamic vinegar
2 bay leaves
¹/₂ teaspoon black peppercorns
1 teaspoon chopped fresh thyme

To clean sardines (which are not usually sold already gutted), make a slit along belly and remove entrails. Rinse fish under running water. Extend the slit far enough that you can grasp backbone with attached bones; discard bones (see page 58). Cut away head and fins, leaving tail intact. Spread fish flat on work surface and dredge in flour on both sides. Heat oil in large skillet. Fry fish in batches on both sides over medium-high heat for 2 to 3 minutes. Remove and drain on rack. Sprinkle both sides with salt and pepper and arrange in large glass or ceramic dish.

Peel and chop onion; peel and crush garlic. Carefully seed red pepper and cut into rings. Heat 1 tablespoon of the oil used for frying in large saucepan. Add onion and garlic and sauté very lightly. Add water, wine, vinegar, bay leaves, red pepper, peppercorns, and thyme and simmer over low heat 2 to 3 minutes. Pour over sardines, cover, and let stand in a cool place for at least 24 hours.

Porgy in Fennel Marinade

Not illustrated

4 servings
8 cleaned whole small porgy (about 3 ounces/80 to 100 g each) or other small saltwater fish
Flour
¹/₄ cup (60 mL) vegetable oil
Salt and freshly ground pepper
1 cup (240 mL) dry white wine
¹/₂ cup (125 mL) water
2 tablespoons wine vinegar
1 large onion
1 lemon
1 bulb fresh fennel
1 large tomato
Salt and freshly ground pepper

Wash the fish; cut away heads and fins. Cut fish open along belly far enough that you can grasp backbone and attached bones and lift them out. Dredge fish in flour and fry on both sides in hot oil 2 to 3 minutes. Season with salt and pepper and drain on paper towels. Arrange cooked fish in large glass or ceramic dish.

Combine wine with water and vinegar in nonaluminum saucepan and bring to boil. Peel onion and lemon; trim fennel. Cut all three into very thin slices, add to wine mixture, and simmer 3 to 4 minutes. Blanch, peel, and seed tomatoes. Cut into cubes and add to marinade. Season with salt and pepper and simmer gently 2 to 3 minutes longer.

Pour marinade over fish, cover, and let stand in a cool place for at least 24 hours.

Mackerel in Wine Marinade

Serve with French bread and butter or with new potatoes boiled in their jackets.

4 servings

4 cleaned whole mackerel (about 10 ounces/300 g each)
2 medium onions
1 large carrot
3 cups (700 mL) dry white wine
1/2 cup (125 mL) wine vinegar
1/2 teaspoon salt
2 whole cloves
3 bay leaves
2 fresh thyme sprigs
Pinch of mace
A few tarragon leaves
1 teaspoon black peppercorns
1 lemon

Carefully wash cleaned mackerel under running water; pat dry. Cut away fins, leaving heads and tails intact.

For the marinade, peel and thinly slice onions. Trim carrot and slice with crinkle cutter. Combine wine and vinegar in large nonaluminum saucepan and bring to boil. Add onion and carrot slices and boil 2 to 3 minutes. Season with salt and add whole spices (cloves, bay leaves, thyme sprig, mace, tarragon leaves, and pepper-

corns); simmer 2 to 3 minutes. Scrub lemon under hot water, slice thinly, and add to marinade.

Arrange mackerel in large flameproof dish and place on top of stove. Pour hot marinade over, cover, and cook over very low heat for 10 to 12 minutes; liquid should barely simmer. Remove from heat and cool fish in liquid, then marinate overnight in refrigerator before serving.

Herring in Herb Marinade

Serve with caraway-flavored boiled potatoes or with whole-grain bread and sweet butter. Not illustrated.

4 servings

4 salt herring (about 8 ounces/250 g each)
1/2 cup (125 mL) water
1 1/2 cups (350 mL) wine vinegar
1 large onion
1/2 teaspoon black peppercorns
2 bay leaves
1 teaspoon mustard seed
1 cup (250 g) crème fraîche
1 fresh chili pepper
3 spicy dill pickles
1 red bell pepper
1/4 cup (20 g) chopped fresh herbs (parsley, chives, lemon balm, tarragon, and lovage or celery leaves)

Soak herring in water to cover generously for 12 hours. Gut fish and wash well. Remove head, tail, fins, and bones; cut herring into pieces.

Combine water and vinegar in large nonaluminum saucepan and bring to boil. Peel and very thinly slice onion and add to saucepan with peppercorns, bay leaves, and mustard seed. Reduce heat and simmer 5 to 6 minutes. Remove from heat and cool.

Whisk crème fraîche into marinade. Halve chili pepper lengthwise, seed and dice finely. Drain pickles well and slice. Cut bell pepper in half, remove seeds, and cut into very thin strips. Mix vegetables and herbs into marinade.

Add herring pieces to marinade, cover and let stand in a cool place for 2 to 3 days for flavors to blend.

METRIC—IMPERIAL CONVERSION TABLE

Note that the recipes in this book feature both U.S. customary and metric measurements. For cooks in Great Britain, Canada, and Australia, note the following information for imperial measurements. If you are familiar with metric measurements, then we recommend you follow those, incorporated into every recipe. If not, then use these conversions to achieve best results. Bear in mind that ingredients such as flour vary greatly and you will have to make some adjustments.

Liquid Measures

The British cup is larger than the American. The Australian cup is smaller than the British but a little larger than the American. Use the following cup measurements for liquids, making the adjustments as indicated.

U.S.	1 cup (236 ml)
British and Canadian	1 cup (284 ml)—adjust measurement to $1/4$ pint + 2 tablespoons
Australian	1 cup (250 ml)—adjust measurement to $1/4$ pint

Weight and Volume Measures

U.S. cooking procedures usually measure certain items by volume, although in other countries these items are often measured by weight. Here are some approximate equivalents for basic items.

	U.S. Customary	Metric	Imperial
Butter	1 cup	250 g	8 ounces
	$1/2$ cup	125 g	4 ounces
	$1/4$ cup	62 g	2 ounces
	1 tablespoon	15 g	$1/2$ ounce
Flour (sifted all-purpose or plain)	1 cup	128 g	$4 1/4$ ounces
	$1/2$ cup	60 g	$2 1/8$ ounces
	$1/4$ cup	32 g	1 ounce
Sugar (caster)	1 cup	240 g	8 ounces
	$1/2$ cup	120 g	4 ounces
	1 tablespoon	15 g	$1/2$ ounce
Chopped vegetables	1 cup	115 g	4 ounces
	$1/2$ cup	60 g	2 ounces
Chopped meats or fish	1 cup	225 g	8 ounces
	$1/2$ cup	110 g	4 ounces

INDEX

Christian Teubner is a highly sought-after photographer specializing in food photography. His work conveys the special magic and fun of cooking, whether he is picturing soups, main courses, or desserts. He again shows his love of cooking in this beautifully illustrated collection of his favorite recipes.